Rain Forests
of the
World

Volume 5
Forest Fire–Iguana

MARSHALL CAVENDISH
NEW YORK • LONDON • TORONTO • SYDNEY

Marshall Cavendish
99 White Plains Road
Tarrytown, New York
10591-9001

Website: www.marshallcavendish.com

Consulting editors: Rolf E. Johnson, Nathan E. Kraucunas

Contributing authors: Theresa Greenaway, Jill Bailey, Michael Chinery, Malcolm Penny, Mike Linley, Philip Steele, Chris Oxlade, Ken Preston-Mafham, Rod Preston-Mafham, Clare Oliver

Discovery Books
    Managing Editor: Paul Humphrey
    Project Editor: Gianna Williams
    Text Editor: Valerie Weber
    Design Concept: Ian Winton
    Page Layout: Keith Williams, Ian Winton
    Cartographer: Stefan Chabluk
    Illustrators: Jim Channell, Stuart Lafford, Christian Webb

Marshall Cavendish
    Editor: Marian Armstrong
    Editorial Director: Paul Bernabeo

(cover) Douc Langur monkey

Editor's Note: Many systems of dating have been used by different cultures throughout history. *Rain Forests of the World* uses B.C.E.. (Before Common Era) and C.E. (Common Era) instead of B.C. (Before Christ) and A.D. (Anno Domini, "In the Year of Our Lord") out of respect for the diversity of the world's peoples.

The publishers would like to thank the following for their permission to reproduce photographs:
238 & 239 Dermot Tatlow/Panos Pictures, 240 Martin Harvey/Natural History Photographic Agency, 241 K. G. Preston-Mafham/Premaphotos Wildlife, 242 Alain Compost/Bruce Coleman, 243 Edward Parker/Oxford Scientific Films, 244 Paul Harrison/Panos Pictures, 245 Nigel J. Dennis/NHPA, 246 James Carmichael Jr./NHPA, 247 Michael Fogden/OSF, 248 Daniel Heuclin/NHPA, 249 Kathie Atkinson/OSF, 250 Alain Compost/Bruce Coleman, 251 K. G. Preston-Mafham/Premaphotos Wildlife, 252 Chris Mattison/Frank Lane Picture Agency, 253 Kevin Schafer/NHPA, 254 Alan Root/OSF, 255 Michael Leach/OSF, 256 Kim Taylor/Bruce Coleman, 257 D. Ellinger/Foto Natura Stock/FLPA, 258 Stan Osolinski/OSF, 259 Gerard Lacz/FLPA,260 Martin Wendler/NHPA, 262 Okapia/OSF, 263 Bernard Regent/Hutchison Picture Library, 264 Mary Plage/Bruce Coleman, 265 E. & D. Hosking/FLPA, 266 Michael Leach/NHPA, 267 Michael Fogden/Bruce Coleman, 268 K. G. Preston-Mafham/ Premaphotos Wildlife, 269 Michael Fogden/Bruce Coleman, 270 K. G. Preston-Mafham/Premaphotos Wildlife, 271 Daniel Heuclin/NHPA, 272 Dr. Eckart Pott/Bruce Coleman, 273 Christer Fredriksson/Bruce Coleman, 275 Michael Gore/FLPA, 276 Martin B. Withers/FLPA, 277 Jeremy Horner/Hutchison Library, 278 Nick Gordon/OSF, 279 S. Errington/Hutchison Library, 280 Martin Harvey/NHPA, 281 Nick Gordon/OSF, 282 Derek Hall/FLPA, 283 Sara Leigh Lewis/Panos Pictures, 285 Chris Mattison/FLPA, 286 Stephen Dalton/NHPA, 287 Michael Fogden/Bruce Coleman, 288 Giacomo Pirozzi/Panos Pictures, 289 Alain Compost/Bruce Coleman, 290 Harold Taylor ABIPP/OSF, 291 Michael Harvey/ Panos Pictures, 292 Hutchison Library, 293 James Morris/Panos Pictures, 294 Joe McDonald/Bruce Coleman, 295 Stephen Dalton/NHPA.

Library of Congress Cataloging-in-Publication Data
Rain forests of the world.
            p. cm.
    Includes bibliographical references and index.
    Contents: v. 1. Africa-bioluminescence—v. 2. Biomass-clear-cutting — v. 3. Climate and weather-emergent — v. 4. Endangered species-food web — v. 5. Forest fire-iguana — v. 6. Indonesia-manatee — v. 7. Mangrove forest-orangutan — v. 8. Orchid-red panda — v. 9. Reforestation-spider — v. 10. Squirrel-Yanomami people — v. 11. Index.
        ISBN 0-7614-7254-1 (set)
        1. Rain forests--Encyclopedias.   I.. Marshall Cavendish Corporation.
    QH86 .R39 2002
    578.734—dc21   2001028460

    ISBN 0-7614-7254-1 (set)
    ISBN 0-7614-7259-2 (vol. 5)

Printed and bound in Italy

07 06 05 04 03 02   6 5 4 3 2 1

Contents

Forest Fire   238
Forest Floor   240
Forestry   242
Frog and Toad   246
Fruit   250
Fungus   252

Galago   254
Gecko   255
Giant Otter   257
Gibbon   258
Global Warming   260
Gorilla   264
Grasshopper, Cricket, and Katydid   267

Herb and Spice   271
Herbivore   273
Homes in the Rain Forest   277
Human Interference   282
Humidity   284
Hummingbird   286
Hunter-Gatherer   288
Hydroelectricity   290

Ibo People   292
Iguana   294

Glossary   296
Index   297

orest fires are terrifying: they create heat and flames, noise from crackling branches and occasionally exploding trees, and above all a sense of complete helplessness. It is not surprising that people who live and work in forests are afraid of them and the damage they can cause.

Small, localized fires can be beneficial to a forest, releasing nutrients that are otherwise trapped in mature trees and shrubs to fertilize the soil and allowing new plants to grow in the increased levels of light. However the vast majority of forest fires are far more destructive.

KEY FACTS

● **People start almost all fires in forests; lightning ignites only 1 or 2 percent.**

● **In 1998 forest fires destroyed 1,235,000 acres (500,000 hectares) of rain forest in Indonesia alone.**

● **Of the three types of forest fire, ground fires are the most dangerous.**

How Fires Start

Natural fires, usually caused by lightning, are rare in tropical rain forests. Scientists say that lightning causes only 1 or 2 percent of forest fires worldwide. People start almost all forest fires, either deliberately or, more often, by accident. In the Tropics the most common form of fire is ignited by people clearing land for farming. In 1998, after a long, dry summer in Indonesia, fires lit to clear forest for agriculture burned out of control. About 1,235,000 acres (500,000 hectares) were destroyed; the resulting smoke caused some of the worst air pollution ever recorded.

Types of Forest Fires

There are three types of forest fires: surface fires, crown fires, and ground fires. Surface fires sweep across the forest floor, burning loose debris such as leaf litter and fallen twigs. Because the fuel is light, surface fires are often short-lived. However, they might burn hot and high enough to set fire to the crowns of trees; if this happens in dry air and a stiff breeze, crown fires might start.

During a crown fire, flames leap from tree to tree high above the ground. Some tropical trees' leaves are coated in a waxy substance that prevents them

Fires sweep across the forests of Indonesia in 1998. The dry summer was caused by the effects of the weather system El Niño.

Firefighters work to control a forest blaze in Indonesia.

from losing too much water, but this burns fiercely, even when the leaves are fresh. Crown fires are the fastest-spreading form of forest fire but the easiest to control by means of firebreaks.

Firebreaks are clear strips cut through the forest, wide enough to prevent flames from jumping across them. Sometimes backfires are used—small controlled fires that create clearings in the forest, removing the fuel before the main fire arrives.

The most dangerous form of forest fire is ground fire, which burns buried dead wood and tree roots below the surface. Ground fires move slowly, but they might smolder for weeks or even months, breaking out again when firefighters are long gone.

Fire Watchers

Ground fires are easier to detect today than they were in the past. Today, airplanes or even satellites can detect heat and report exactly where fires are. The firefighting crews can then move in, dousing the fire with water either from the ground or from planes.

Preventing Fires

Forest fires can be prevented by mapping the forest to identify places where the risk is greatest and making permanent firebreaks. Small naturally occurring fires can be allowed to burn so that dead wood does not accumulate.

Check these out:

- Cattle Ranching
- Forestry
- National Park
- Slash and Burn

IN FOCUS

Danger of Fire

Visitors to forest reserves are warned about the risk of fire. Cooking fires and campfires are banned except in specially prepared places. All litter must be taken home, of course, as well as broken glass that could magnify sunlight and start flames. Smoking, which is dangerous at all times for health reasons, is doubly dangerous in the forest since a discarded cigarette butt can start a forest fire.

The floor of a tropical rain forest is a dark, damp place. Mosses and ferns grow on the ground, along with a few flowering plants that can withstand the deep shade. Many have dark leaves that help them absorb the dim light more efficiently than lighter leaves would. Some tree seedlings sprout on the forest floor and wait for a light gap to appear; this happens when old trees fall and enough light reaches the ground.

KEY FACTS

● **Many rain forests have been destroyed in order to extract the aluminum ore found under the soil.**

● **One kind of rain forest cup fungi decorates the forest floor with what looks like pieces of red, orange, pink, and yellow plastic.**

● **In many rain forest areas, termites are the most numerous of all creatures.**

Scavenging Leaves and Nuts

Many of the leaves that fall to the ground do not stay there for long. Hordes of scavenging creatures that live on the forest floor consume most of them immediately. These scavengers include snails, cockroaches, beetles, millipedes, and the most numerous of all creatures in many rain forest areas, termites. Social insects, termites live in colonies that may contain hundreds of thousands of individuals. They scour the surrounding ground for food, collecting fallen twigs and seeds as well as leaves.

Birds enjoy the abundant seeds that litter the forest floor; mice and other rodents may join the feast. The squirrel-like agoutis of South America can crack open the hard fruits of Brazil nuts. They listen for the crash of a falling fruit, which looks like a wooden baseball and weighs about 4 pounds (1.8 kg). They must gnaw through the outer coat of the ball, as well as through the hard shells of the many individual seeds inside it.

Leaves, twigs, and seeds not eaten by animals are attacked by fungi and microscopic bacteria, and they quickly rot away in the warm, damp atmosphere.

Few small plants can grow on the forest floor—there is just not enough light.

This dung beetle will bury its ball of coati dung as a food store for its grubs. Without dung beetles and other insects, the forest floor would be littered with animal wastes.

Nourished by this rotting material, some weird and colorful mushrooms spring up on the rain forest floor, such as the cup fungi of the *Phillipsia* family, which look like pieces of red, orange, pink, and yellow plastic on the forest floor.

Prowling Predators

Beetles, centipedes, hunting spiders, and many other small predators prowl through the leaves and feast on the scavengers. Scorpions and the similar whip scorpions lurk among the leaves or under fallen bark and snatch passing animals with their big claws. Many birds, including colorful pittas and jewel thrushes, also scour the forest floor, feeding on insects and other small animals.

However, the most numerous and important predators on the rain forest floor are the ants. Driver ants or army ants roam the forest floor in long columns, killing anything in their path. They butcher their victims with their huge jaws.

Even leopards and jaguars get out of the way of these killers. Ants of various kinds also eat carrion, helping to clear the forest floor of dead animals.

Larger animals cannot find much to eat on the ground. They stay mainly in the dense undergrowth along the riverbanks and in clearings where trees have fallen.

Rain Forest Soil

Rain forest soils are formed by the breakdown of the underlying rocks over millions of years. Most rain forest soils are only 8 to 12 inches (20 to 30 cm) deep, but some are over 9 feet (3 m) deep. Most rain forest soils tend to be rich brown or reddish because the heavy rainfall washes many of the minerals to lower levels, leaving insoluble iron and aluminum compounds at the surface. In many places the rain forests have been destroyed in order to extract the aluminum ore. Rain forest soil is acidic and not very fertile because the useful minerals leach out and are redeposited below the level of the plant roots.

Check these out:

- Ant ● Bacteria ● Beetle ● Bird
- ● Decomposer ● Fungus ● Millipede
- ● Parrot, Macaw, and Parakeet ● Termite

IN FOCUS

Clay Soils

Calcium-rich clays occur in some parts of the Amazonian rain forest, and they attract large numbers of macaws and parrots. The birds eat the clay, which is thought to absorb or neutralize the poisons in some of the fruits that they eat.

Forestry

Until recently forestry was concerned only with growing and harvesting as many trees as possible. However, when people realized that forests were being destroyed faster than they could recover, the style of forestry changed. Today forestry has become the science of developing and managing woodlands for the benefit of local people and industry. This may still sometimes mean just producing good timber, but it usually has a much wider aim, working for wildlife and habitat conservation and simply preserving the beauty of forests so that people can visit them for recreation. Forests are now known to be important for preventing erosion and protecting water supplies, as well as reducing carbon pollution in the air, and forestry must take those goals into account as well.

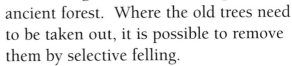

KEY FACTS

● **Modern tree-planting machines can plant 30,000 to 40,000 seedlings in one day.**

● **Areas where trees have been completely felled take decades to recover naturally.**

Forest Products

Most of the products people need can be produced just as well by trees grown on plantations as by those taken from mature rain forests. Pulp to make paper, wood chips to make building materials, and timber for building and carpentry can all be made from small, young trees. The huge old trees, the glory of the forest, provide valuable hardwood that is used for furniture and cabinetmaking and is rightly very expensive. However, the main work of the forester in producing wood can be done without interfering with the remaining stands of ancient forest. Where the old trees need to be taken out, it is possible to remove them by selective felling.

Clear-Cutting Versus Selective Felling

Clear-cutting, where large tracts of forest are completely cut down, is still practiced in some parts of the world, especially in South America, where it is used to open up land for ranching and farming. However, more and more alternative methods of logging are being used. Selective felling—choosing either single trees or small groups to fell—prevents erosion by leaving

If planting is done by small groups of people soon after the forest is felled, as here in Indonesia, there is a good chance that the forest will eventually recover.

Helicopter logging in New Zealand. Lifting timber out of the forest like this is expensive, but it prevents damaging other trees in the area.

some roots to hold down the soil and allows the forest to regenerate naturally in the clearings that remain. Even then, felled trees can fall against neighboring ones and damage them, unless the trees are removed with helicopters, which is very expensive.

Natural Regeneration

Natural regeneration means allowing saplings to grow from seeds that have fallen from mature trees around the clearings created by felling. If the clearings are not too big, it works well; after all, this is what happens in a wild forest following a windstorm or a fire. Natural regeneration follows a cycle called succession, in which different plants grow in the cleared area until they are overtaken by others. In a typical succession, small herbs grow up first, followed by shrubs, and finally by taller trees. The trees compete for light until the biggest of them win, forming the "climax community" of the forest, where no further changes take place and all fast-growing saplings have been replaced by forest giants.

Natural regeneration takes decades, so foresters sometimes shorten the succession by transplanting climax tree

IN FOCUS

Fire Prevention

Natural fires are rare in the rain forest because the mass of damp vegetation is unlikely to burn even when it is struck by lightning. However, fire is often used to clear the forest for farmland, and foresters have to try to control it by cutting corridors known as firebreaks.

seedlings immediately and keeping the ground clear of competing plants while the trees grow up. This process is called artificial regeneration, or silviculture.

Artificial Regeneration

In artificial regeneration, foresters plant seedlings, not seeds. This is because seeds are important food for the mice, squirrels, and birds that live in the forest, and the aim of the foresters is to grow trees, not feed wildlife. For replanting in the Tropics, the seedlings are usually grown in containers, so they have a ball of soil around their roots that makes them easier to plant. Today, machines help foresters plant seedling trees.

A modern tree-planting machine can plant 30,000 to 40,000 seedlings per day, with only four people running it. This is

Agroforestry can make use of the forest without felling all the trees. Here, in Colombia, coffee bushes are growing under banana plants.

an amazingly efficient way of replanting large areas of cleared ground, but the heavy machine can damage the soil of the forest floor as it works. Deep, soft leaf litter that has accumulated over the centuries can easily be squashed and compacted until it no longer holds water and is unsuitable for growing anything.

An alternative method is for people to plant the seedlings by hand. Although slow, it gives work to many people, and their feet do less harm to the forest floor than the wheels and tracks of the machines. In many tropical areas, planting by hand is seen as the best way to repair the damage done by logging. It has other advantages too: local people feel they are in charge of what is happening to their forest.

Agroforestry

Growing crops among trees is called agroforestry. Crops such as bananas, cacao, sweet potatoes, and corn in South America, or yams and cassavas in Africa,

In tree nurseries in Madagascar, local species of trees are cultivated, ready for replanting. In this way, people are working to restore the damaged forests.

can be grown this way. The trees may be planted around the edge of farmland, where they act as a windbreak and can also be trimmed to produce animal feed and firewood without killing them. If the trimming is done carefully, under the guidance of experienced foresters, the trees will continue to grow until they become full-sized forest trees. Sometimes the trees are planted in rows with the crops between them and allowed to grow until the canopy closes high above and no more crops can be grown. The regenerated forest can then be exploited for timber or left to develop into mature forest, though this may take 100 years or more.

These methods of forestry are designed to enable people to use the land for crops while it is growing back into forest. The farmers benefit by having the crops, fuel, and animal feed, but there are much wider benefits, too.

Visitors to the Forest

By living in the forest instead of removing it, the people preserve the habitat for wildlife, and this in turn attracts visitors—eco-tourists—who bring money with them to pay for services such as guest houses and guides. This is the recreational side of forestry, in which the forest earns money for local people without their having to destroy it.

When large numbers of people visit, forestry skills are needed to protect the forest from the effects of those visitors. By making clear paths and trails, the forester can make sure that visitors do not ramble everywhere, trampling the ground

vegetation and damaging the delicate forest floor. Providing bridges helps keep streams clean. Forest guides or wardens can give advice and information and make sure that people stick to the rules. Building work and guiding provide jobs for local people, increasing their sense of the value of the intact forest, rather than seeing it simply as a source of money from fallen trees.

Check these out:
● Careers ● Clear-Cutting ● Exploitation
● Forest Fire ● Human Interference
● Logging ● National Park
● Tourism

IN FOCUS

Seed Orchards

Seed orchards are stands of especially good specimens of trees from which the seeds are collected to be grown in containers, ready to be planted in the forest to replace trees that have been cut down. The forester's job is to make sure that the right species of trees are planted in the appropriate part of the forest.

There are nearly 4,500 species of frogs and toads found throughout the world from tropical rain forests to deserts to alpine meadows. However, without doubt, the frogs' stronghold is the tropical rain forest. It is ideally suited to them—warm, moist, and crawling with insect food.

Biologically speaking, frogs and toads are very similar. Frogs and toads, along with caecilians (which resemble worms), newts, and salamanders, form the group of animals known as amphibians. Typically these are thin-skinned, moisture-loving vertebrates that normally undergo a metamorphosis from a water-dwelling tadpole stage to an air-breathing terrestrial stage.

Frogs and toads form a group of amphibians called the anurans (uh-NYUHR-uhns). They have no tails as adults, and they have larger hind legs than front legs, which help them jump. Possessing large, round, bulging eyes, many species are nocturnal. Frogs and toads feed mostly on insects, although some of the larger types capture prey as large as mice and snakes. Unlike other amphibians, male frogs and toads normally have a large vocal sac that produces a loud call or croak to attract females. Many species secrete toxins in their skin to deter predators, and some of these can be highly poisonous.

KEY FACTS

● **The world's smallest and largest frogs live in rain forests.**

● **The poison dart frog produces a toxin that can cause death in humans in a matter of minutes.**

● **Cane toads were introduced into farmland cleared from Australian rain forests to eat sugarcane pests and now are a major pest themselves.**

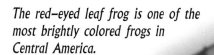

The red-eyed leaf frog is one of the most brightly colored frogs in Central America.

Frogs in Trees

Only a few rain forest frogs are aquatic; the majority are terrestrial, and of these, many live in trees. Tree frogs have specially modified toe pads that enable them to climb among the branches. Each toe ends in a disk that forms a sort of suction cup. Frogs can cling to leaves with just one toe.

A female rough–skinned poison dart frog carries her single tadpole for several days before depositing it into a small pool of water.

Some frog species never come down to the ground. They lay their eggs in sticky masses on branches overhanging a pool or stream. When the tadpoles hatch, they wriggle free and flop into the water below to continue their development.

Some of these tree frogs are brightly colored, such as the red-eyed leaf frog from the rain forests of Costa Rica. It has bright red eyes, orange feet, a green body, and blue and yellow markings on its sides. Females can reach a length of 4 inches (10 cm), while males usually reach only half that size.

Colorful Poisoners

Poison dart frogs are even more vividly colorful, being blue, red, yellow, green, or orange—all warning colors. They live primarily on the ground throughout Central and South America, only occasionally climbing the lower reaches of the trees. They rarely exceed 1 to 2 inches (2.5 to 5 cm), but despite their small size, these are some of the most poisonous animals known to exist. The toxin in their skin, used to deter predators from eating them, is lethal if it enters an animal's bloodstream through sores in its mouth or ulcers in its stomach. It can cause death in a human in a matter of minutes and in a monkey in a matter of seconds. Local Indians in Colombia use these frogs' secretions to tip their blow darts.

IN FOCUS

A Tiny Hopper

One of the world's smallest frogs lives in the rain forests of eastern Brazil. *Psyllophryne didactyla* is only ⅖ in. (1 cm) long when fully grown. Difficult to find in the leaf litter of the forest, it is a fast jumper. It feeds on tiny insects such as springtails.

247

A Giant Frog

The world's largest frog lives in the rain forests of Cameroon in western Africa. The goliath frog can reach a body length of 2½ ft. (76 cm) with its legs outstretched—and can weigh 8 lb. (3.6 kg). It is big enough to eat mice, rats, and other frogs. Local people hunt the goliath frog for food, but they also use its hipbone as a lucky charm.

Most species of poison dart frogs are also careful parents. The males or females, depending on the species, carry from 1 to 20 tadpoles on their backs for several days before depositing them in a suitable pool.

Aquatic Frogs and Toads

The rain forests of Central and South America are important habitats for frogs and toads of all sorts, some very bizarre. One of the strangest is an aquatic species, the Surinam toad. It lives in rivers and lakes throughout the rain forest of northern South America. About the size of a saucer, it is completely flat. This, combined with its triangular head and coloration, makes it look just like a dead leaf on the riverbed. There, it sits motionless, with its front legs outstretched, waiting for fish and insects to come within range of its sensitive toes. When they do, it crams them into its mouth with lightning speed. Enormous webs stretch between the toes on its large hind feet, making it a powerful swimmer. Although aquatic, the Surinam toad must surface every few minutes to take in a gulp of air.

Another unusual feature of the Surinam toad is the way it breeds. The male seizes the female around her waist. They then do a somersault in the water. She lays two or three eggs that he fertilizes. The eggs then roll down onto her back, where they stick and begin to be engulfed in a spongy material. When she has laid 60 or 70 eggs, the pair separates. The tadpoles undergo their entire development in individual pouches on her back. After about two months, these pouches burst open, and perfectly formed little frogs swim away.

Some frogs in these forests have become completely independent of water. Whistling frogs simply lay eggs under leaves. The eggs hatch out as tiny frogs; the young undergo the entire tadpole stage within the egg.

Asian Frogs

The rain forests of Asia are home to some strange frogs, too. The Malaysian horned frog is shaped and colored to mimic a dead leaf, right down to the leaf veins on its back and stalks on the end of its nose and over each eye. It is almost impossible to spot on the forest floor. High in the trees live dozens of types of tree frogs. One of them, known as the flying frog, has webbed front feet as well as back; when it leaps out of a tree, it uses these to form little parachutes that effectively break its fall. These frogs mate in the trees and lay their eggs in a frothy mass that the pair whip up with their back feet. The nest is then wrapped in nearby leaves. The eggs hatch a week or so later, and tadpoles drop into the water below.

Giant Toads

One of the largest toads in the rain forest is the giant toad, which can reach a body length of over 10 inches (25 cm) and a weight of up to 5 pounds (2.2 kg). Its body is covered in warts. Just behind its eyes lies a pair of large glands. A toxic secretion is produced from these and other parts of its body if it is attacked by a predator, such as a coati or dog. The substance is so toxic that it causes instant pain, vomiting, and in some cases even death.

The male giant toad's rattling call can be heard echoing from riverbanks throughout the forest, especially after heavy rain. The female lays strings of up to 20,000 eggs. The tiny toads are a mere one third of an inch (8 mm) in length when they leave the water and may take 10 years to reach full size.

The giant toad is also known as the cane toad because it has been introduced to warm climates all over the world (especially Australia) in an attempt to control the cane beetle, a pest of sugarcane crops. Unfortunately other animals of the Australian rain forest are now in danger of being poisoned by the toad, which, in the absence of natural predators, is establishing itself well. Efforts are now being made to reduce its numbers there.

A giant toad, or cane toad, introduced into the forests of Australia to control the cane beetle, eats a frog that is native to those forests. The cane toad has become a major pest of Australian rain forests.

Check these out:

- Amazonia
- Amphibian
- Australia
- Biodiversity
- Bromeliad
- Central America
- Courtship
- Epiphyte

Fruit

If seeds were to just drop from the parent tree onto the ground below, few would ever have a chance to grow. Those not eaten by ground-dwelling creatures would have to compete with the parent tree for light and nutrients. So trees have evolved with ingenious ways of having their seeds transported away from the parent to another part of the forest. One of these ways is to bear fruit.

A fruit is basically a container for a plant's seeds. Different kinds of fruit attract different animals, which take the seeds and deposit them far from their parent plant.

KEY FACTS

● **Fruits develop after the flowers have been pollinated; seeds develop inside the fruits.**

● **Birds are attracted to brightly colored juicy fruits. Fruit bats and other mammals take little notice of colors; smells usually lure them in.**

Attracting Animals

Most rain forest plants produce juicy fruits with bright colors to attract birds, monkeys, and other animals. White or other pale-colored fruits show up in the dark and tend to attract fruit bats and other nocturnal mammals. Smelly fruits usually attract mammals rather than birds because birds do not have a good sense of smell.

The animals eat the flesh, which contains sugars, other carbohydrates, and various proteins, and then scatter the seeds, either by spitting them out if they are too large to swallow or eating them with the fruit and then passing them out whole in their droppings. As the animals move away from the tree to consume the fruit, seeds are dispersed away from the parent plant. Seeds that

The rambutan (ram–BOO–tehn) grows in the forests of Southeast Asia. Inside its shaggy red coat is a soft white flesh.

Breadfruit

Breadfruit was once the staple food of people living on various islands in the Pacific Ocean. About as big as a soccer ball, the fruit has a rough skin and is full of starch. When sliced up and roasted, it is similar to bread. One breadfruit tree produces enough fruit to feed one person for a year.

are swallowed whole usually have very tough coats; most of them pass through the animals' digestive systems undamaged. The animal's droppings surrounding the seeds act like a fertilizer and give the young seedlings a good start in life.

Ripe fruits are available in the rain forests throughout the year. They are a major source of food for rain forest animals, and many birds eat nothing else. Figs are particularly important for birds and monkeys because they are a rich source of vitamins and minerals, especially iron. Hundreds of different kinds of figs grow in the forests, although most of them are quite small and nothing like the figs that humans eat. Many have a bitter taste.

Fruits for Humans

Although rain forest fruits are good for birds and monkeys, not many of them are good for people to eat. Inhabitants of the rain forest know exactly which ones they can and cannot eat. Some of the best fruits, especially bananas native to Southeast Asia and pineapples from South America, are now cultivated on a large scale.

Originally from Central America, the avocado is a large, tough-skinned berry containing one very large seed and a mass of oily, butterlike flesh. It also contains a lot of protein. The resplendent quetzal, one of the most striking birds in Central America, plucks avocados from the trees in flight. These wild fruits are much smaller than cultivated avocados, and the bird can just about get one into its beak.

The Smelly Durian

The durian (DUHR-ee-uhn) is a large tree native to Southeast Asia. Its spiky fruits weigh about 7 pounds (3 kg). Walking under a durian tree can be a smelly experience—the skin of the fruit smells like rotting fish, but it attracts orangutans and many other animals. These creatures know that a deliciously sweet, creamy pulp surrounds the seeds inside the fruit. Local people also enjoy this pulp, which tastes like a mixture of caramel and banana. Durians are cultivated on a large scale in Southeast Asia.

Check these out:
● Flowering Plant ● Food ● Herb and Spice ● Pollination ● Seed

Over 100,000 species of fungi (FUN-jie) grow throughout the world, and they play a vital role in recycling organic material in the tropical rain forest. What we recognize as mushrooms and toadstools (which are forms of fungi) are just the fruiting bodies of a whole network of thin, transparent hyphae (HIE-fee), or tubes, that actually form the plant itself. Fungi do not possess chlorophyll like other plants, so they do not need light and thrive in dark, damp places. Thus the rain forest is an ideal environment for fungi.

KEY FACTS

● **A single nest of leaf-cutter ants may contain several hundred fungus gardens, each containing an 8 to 12 in. (20 to 30 cm) in diameter fungus colony.**

● **Most fungi in the rain forest are decomposers.**

Three Types of Fungi

Different types of fungi find nourishment in three ways. Saprophytes live on dead plant or animal matter, their hyphae penetrating decomposing organic matter such as dead leaves, dead animals, and animal waste. Parasites are fungi that consume living organisms, either plant or animal, causing infections such as "rust" in plants. Finally there are those fungi that live by forming an association with another plant that benefits both species. Lichens (LIE-kuhns) are a symbiosis, or mutually beneficial association, between an alga and a fungus: the alga, a tiny plant or plantlike organism, possesses chlorophyll and can produce food in the presence of sunlight, while the fungus forms the actual structure of the lichen.

The majority of fungi in the rain forests belong to the first group of decomposers. They play a vital role in breaking down dead plants and animals and releasing their nutrients, making these available for other plants and animals.

The fruiting body of the fungus (the familiar mushroom or toadstool) grows in order to produce millions of spores that disperse and grow into new fungi. These spores can be dispersed by wind, water droplets, or animals. In the Northern Hemisphere, these are prolific in autumn when it is warm and damp and dead plant matter abounds. In the tropical rain forest, these conditions prevail all year round, so fungi can be found at any time. Rain forest fungi come in a bewildering

The cookeina fungus produces tiny pink cuplike fruiting bodies, usually on rotting logs.

The maiden's veil stinkhorn gets its name from the strange netlike structure that grows around its stalk and from the foul smell it produces.

On dead or dying tree trunks in both Asian and South American rain forests, a fungus called *Marasmius* forms dozens of tiny, delicate, off-white umbrellas with gills on their undersides, laden with spores that fall out when ripe. *Cookeina tricholoma* is a cup fungus that is often found growing on dead nibung palm trees in the warm, wet rain forests of Indonesia. This fungus forms tiny cups covered in fine white hairs.

Check these out:

⬤ Ant ⬤ Decomposer ⬤ Forest Floor
⬤ Lichen ⬤ Moss ⬤ Parasite

variety of forms, including smelly stinkhorns, candle snuff fungi, inky caps, and puffballs.

Cups, Umbrellas, and Stinkhorns

In the forests of Papua New Guinea grows the maiden's veil stinkhorn. This fungus forms egglike balls, known as devil's eggs, in the humus layers of the tropical forest. (The humus layer lies above the soil and consists of decomposing vegetation.) Inside the egg is a complete, folded-up mushroom. This egg then starts to rupture, and the head of the fungus emerges, covered in a black, sticky, smelly mass of spores. The stem then grows and lifts this head 5 inches (13 cm) above the forest floor, and an ornate white lacy "veil" unfolds from under the head. All this occurs in the space of a few hours. The smelly, sticky spores attract insects such as flies that land on the fungus. The spores stick to the insects' feet, and they fly away, transporting the spores as they go.

IN FOCUS

Fungus Farms

One of the most remarkable of the rain forest fungi is virtually never seen. It exists only in the nests of leaf-cutter ants in the rain forests of Central and South America. These ants are often seen forming lines on the forest floor, carrying pieces of leaves and flowers over their head. They take this plant material to their nest where it is chopped and chewed by the workers and used as a food for the fungus gardens tended by the ants. A single nest may contain several hundred gardens, each containing a fungus colony 8 to 12 in. (20 to 30 cm) in diameter. The ants in turn feed on the swollen tips of the hyphae, which are their staple diet. When new queen ants emerge and leave to form new colonies, each one flies off with a tiny parcel of fungus in a special pouch under her head.

Small and furry with huge eyes, big pink ears, and a long furry tail, galagos (guh-LAE-goes) live in the forests of Africa. These mammals are sometimes called bush babies because their loud cries sound like children yelling.

Galagos live in small groups of sisters, daughters, and their young with a single adult male who mates with all the females. The females produce one baby or twins twice a year. Once grown, male galagos live in small bachelor groups or on their own, but they try to replace the males in family groups whenever they get the opportunity.

Night Vision

Galagos spend the day asleep in a tree hole or in a nest of green leaves in the fork of a tree, emerging at night to feed. Their huge eyes gather what little light there is; their sight is aided by a reflective layer at the back of the eye. As the angle of the light changes, the color of their eyes changes from deep yellow to a luminous greenish blue.

Their large ears give them extremely acute hearing. The ears are very flexible; the galago can turn them in different directions to follow sounds. It can also turn its head through almost 180 degrees, so it can look over its back.

With lightning-quick reactions, galagos can catch moths and grasshoppers that fly past. Some kinds of galagos have very long fingers for digging grubs out of tree bark. They also eat fruit, nuts, snails, and tree frogs; some large galago species eat lizards, eggs, and chicks.

Leaving Messages

Galagos have an unusual way of keeping in touch with each other in the dark. They urinate on their paws, leaving a smelly trail wherever they go. Special chemicals in their urine tell other galagos who they are, where their territory is, and how long ago they passed by.

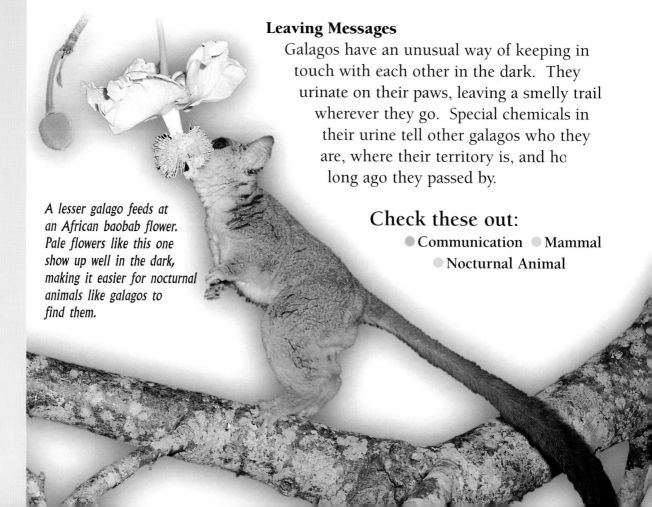

A lesser galago feeds at an African baobab flower. Pale flowers like this one show up well in the dark, making it easier for nocturnal animals like galagos to find them.

Check these out:
● Communication ● Mammal
● Nocturnal Animal

Geckos are a type of lizard and belong to the reptile family. Most are nocturnal and have large eyes. There are over 900 species found throughout the warmer parts of the world, living in habitats ranging from hot deserts to warm tropical rain forests.

KEY FACTS

● **Geckos, like some other lizards, can shed their tail when attacked by predators.**

● **The largest gecko in the world is 24 in. (61 cm) long, but no living specimen has been seen since one was caught in New Zealand's rain forests over 100 years ago.**

Unusual Lizards

Geckos are distinguished from other lizards by two special features. Unlike most lizards, which have eyelids and can blink, the gecko has a large transparent shield covering each eye, just like a snake. Most lizards clean their eyes by blinking, but the gecko cannot do this; instead it washes each eye with its large flat tongue. Depending on the species, the pupil of the eye can expand or contract either vertically, horizontally, or in a circle. At night its pupils open wide to collect as much light as possible.

The gecko's feet are also unusual. It has flattened toes with rows and rows of microscopic hooked hairs covering the bottom; these hairs seek out tiny crevices. Dwarf geckos even have them on the tip of their tails. Their grip is so good they can walk along the underside of leaves. They can even crawl up windows and along ceilings.

Geckos are among the few lizards that have a voice. In most tropical parts of the world, they are called chitchats.

IN FOCUS

Parachuting Geckos

The flying gecko lives in the forests of Malaysia. It has a flattened tail and flaps of skin on the side of its head and body. When the gecko leaps out of a tree to escape a predator such as a snake, the flaps form a parachute and help control the gecko's descent to the ground.

Most geckos lay one or two hard-shelled eggs. These are sticky when fresh, and the gecko glues them to the underside of bark or inside a tree hole.

American Geckos

The turnip-tailed gecko lives in the rain forests of Central and South America. About 6 inches (15 cm) long, it feeds on moths, termites, and other insects. Its thick tail can store fat, allowing it to live for long periods without food.

Often living close by is another species of gecko, the naked-fingered gecko. These are much smaller and are among the few diurnal species of geckos. They can often be seen running up and down tree trunks in daylight, especially around forest clearings. They do not have the specialized feet of their relatives; instead they have sharp claws. They feed on insects, especially termites.

Madagascan Geckos

Madagascar is home to a spectacular group of rain forest geckos, the green day geckos. They are diurnal and among the most brightly colored of all lizards. They range in size from 3 inches (8 cm) to over 8 inches (20 cm). They have small eyes, since they feed in daylight. Excellent climbers, they spend most of their time on leaves and flowers, where they are well camouflaged. In addition to insects, these geckos will eat nectar and pollen.

Madagascar is also home to the bizarre leaf-tailed geckos. These lizards are nocturnal and live mainly on tree trunks, where their mottled brown skin camouflages them perfectly. Over 12 inches (30 cm) in length, their main features are their flattened tail and fringes of skin around their sides and lower jaw. As they sleep, leaf-tailed geckos mold themselves to trees so they do not cast a shadow.

Giant Geckos

The tokay, one of the world's largest geckos, lives in Malaysian rain forests. This 14-inch (35-cm) monster gets its name from its call, "tok-kay," which can be heard in forests throughout the night. Gray with orange spots, this gecko has a fearsome bite. It feeds on a variety of insects and small vertebrates, including other geckos.

Check these out:
- Lizard
  - Nocturnal Animal
  - Reptile

The Madagascan green day gecko uses its large flat tongue to clean its eyes.

Giant Otter

The giant otter is the world's largest otter. It grows up to almost 6 feet (2 m) long, including a tail 2 feet (60 cm) long, and can weigh 66 pounds (30 kg). Superbly adapted to underwater hunting, it lives in the slow-moving rivers and lakes of the Amazonian rain forest, feeding mainly on fish, supplemented by waterbirds, eggs, and small mammals.

Built for Water

The otter's sleek, streamlined body is flexible, and its short legs and large webbed feet act like paddles for swimming. A large flattened tail helps it to push against the water and also does duty as a rudder. The animal can close its ears and nostrils while under water. Out of the water, its thick, water-repelling fur dries quickly.

Hunting mainly by touch, the giant otter feels in the mud for fish with its sensitive paws. Long whiskers on its snout, mouth, and elbows help it sense water movements made by prey. Once close enough, the otter seizes its victim in its mouth.

Giant otters live and hunt in family groups of up to 20 animals. They hunt for about an hour several times a day, then rest on the riverbank while they digest each meal.

The giant otter uses its paws to hunt and eat. Its large whiskers help it feel its way under water.

Otter Communication

When together, giant otters will chatter to each other. When farther apart, they will chirp to keep in touch; giant otters' loud calls travel a long way. If angry, they growl.

Otters also communicate by scent, leaving smelly signals (spraints) in droppings and urine, which they smear over leaves and twigs around their territory.

Giant otters also make a huge, smelly statement about their territory. Stripping away the vegetation, they clear a large semicircle on the riverbank, up to 23 feet (7 m) long and 20 feet (6 m) wide. They use this as a communal latrine. The otters use their front paws to make a smelly mixture of droppings and urine, then trample it into the ground. The smell lasts for weeks, and the cleared ground can be seen from far off.

Check these out:
● Amazonia ● Endangered Species ● Mammal ● River

Gibbon

Gibbons live in the tropical rain forests of Southeast Asia, in Laos, Vietnam, the Malay Peninsula, Thailand, Borneo, and Java. Slender, fruit-eating primates with long limbs and thick hair, gibbons live almost exclusively in trees, only rarely venturing to the ground. They move mainly by brachiation (brae-kee-AE-shuhn), swinging through the trees by their hands. They walk easily on their hind legs on thick branches high in the trees.

Gibbon Families

Unlike the great apes, male and female gibbons are about the same size; age and sex are distinguished by the color of their coats and face patterns. Gibbons live in family groups and pair for life. Each family has a territory that it defends against other gibbons. A family of gibbons spends two or three hours a day moving around its territory and about three hours feeding on soft fruit and young leaves. In the rain forest, gibbons can find food at all times of the year. Knowing their territory so well, they choose which trees to visit—and when— to find the best fruit. They test their food before they pick it, leaving unripe fruits to be picked later.

Gibbons produce a single baby every two or three years. Young gibbons stay with the family group until they are about eight years old, so a typical family will have two or three offspring of various ages. When the young are fully grown, at about six years old, they remain very friendly to their brothers and sisters, are alternately friendly and aggressive to their father, and avoid their mother completely. Gradually their awkwardness with their father makes them leave the family to start one of their own.

The young males look for a mate by singing, wandering through the forest until they find an

Siamangs live on the Malay Peninsula and in Sumatra. They are the closest-knit of all gibbons, and members of a family seldom feed more than 30 ft. (10 m) apart.

With such acrobatic parents, a young gibbon must be able to hang on tightly to its mother as she swings through the branches with other members of the family.

unattached female from another family. The young females wander about listening. When they meet, they do not necessarily form a pair at once; there is a period of courtship, after which they might separate in order to find different partners.

Singing

Singing is an important part of a gibbon family's life. Pairs sing beautiful duets, often harmonizing together. Adults have throat sacs that amplify these calls, so they carry over long distances.

Although its main purpose is to advertise and defend the family territory, there is growing evidence that singing strengthens the bond between the parents and helps keep the family together. Most families sing every day for about 15 minutes, though some species sing less often. After the whole family has warmed up, the parents then sing their duet, followed by "great calls" from the female. These are long trilling howls, accompanied by much thrashing of branches by the whole family. This way their neighbors can be in no doubt that they are in residence and that the female will not tolerate any other females approaching her mate, even though they might have been attracted by his fine voice.

Gibbons under Threat

Gibbons have few enemies, natural or human; the forest people venerate them as good spirits, almost as cousins, because of their upright posture and expressive faces. The only real threat to their survival is the steady destruction of the rain forests that are their only home.

IN FOCUS

Kloss's Gibbon

The Kloss's gibbon is one of four primate species that are found only on the Mentawai Islands, off the coast of Sumatra. Female Kloss's gibbons often give their "great call" in midair as they leap from one branch to another. Kloss's gibbons are negatively affected by even small levels of logging in their limited habitat.

Check these out:

● Ape ● Communication ● Locomotion
● Natural Selection ● Primate

Weather records show that the average temperature of our atmosphere increased by about 0.9°F (0.5°C) during the 20th century, and it is expected to keep rising. This gradual increase in the average temperature of the earth's atmosphere is known as global warming.

Two human activities are thought to be responsible for this increase. They are the burning of fuels (wood, coal, gas, and oil) and deforestation, especially that of tropical rain forests. If we cannot stop global warming, it will eventually have a major and possibly disastrous effect on the world's climates and sea levels.

KEY FACTS

● **The major greenhouse gas contributing to global warming is carbon dioxide.**

● **To make up for increased levels of greenhouse gases, we would have to plant a rain forest the size of Australia.**

The Greenhouse Effect

The earth's atmosphere traps heat in a similar way to the glass of a greenhouse. This effect is called the greenhouse effect. Light and heat from the sun (in the form of infrared radiation) travel through space and hit the earth. Clouds and dust in the atmosphere reflect some light and heat, but most passes through and reaches the surface, which warms up. The warm ground and sea radiate

A clearing in the rain forests of southern Brazil. The greenhouse gas carbon dioxide was released into the atmosphere when the rain forest trees were burned.

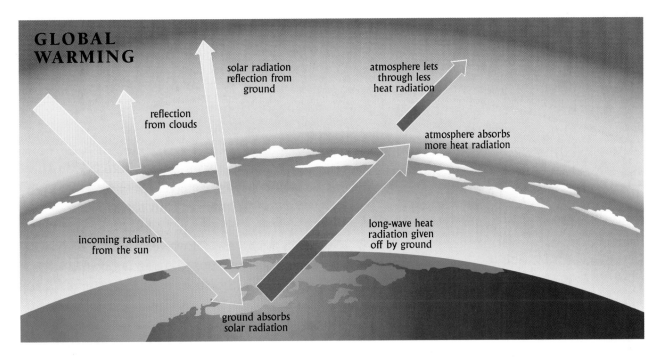

GLOBAL WARMING

solar radiation reflection from ground

atmosphere lets through less heat radiation

reflection from clouds

atmosphere absorbs more heat radiation

incoming radiation from the sun

long-wave heat radiation given off by ground

ground absorbs solar radiation

the heat back into the atmosphere but in a slightly different form. In this different form, it is absorbed by certain atmospheric gases that, in turn, heat up the whole atmosphere. Without the greenhouse effect, all the sun's heat would escape directly back into space, and the earth would be an icy, lifeless world.

Greenhouse Gases

The main greenhouse gases include water vapor, carbon dioxide, methane, nitrogen oxides, and chlorofluorocarbons. The higher the amount of greenhouse gases in the atmosphere, the more the sun's heat is trapped, and the higher the overall temperature of the atmosphere becomes.

Carbon dioxide makes up only about 0.03 percent of the earth's atmosphere, but it is the major greenhouse gas. It moves both in and out of the atmosphere as part of the carbon cycle. For example, plants absorb carbon dioxide as they photosynthesize to make food, and animals release it during respiration. For millions of years, the amount of carbon dioxide taken from and released into the

atmosphere balanced out, so there was no overall change. However, human activities are now upsetting this balance. Carbon dioxide in the atmosphere is increasing.

Analysis of the air in tiny bubbles trapped in ice formed hundreds of years ago in the polar ice caps shows how the carbon dioxide content of the atmosphere has changed. In the 17th century, it was about 0.028 percent (or 280 parts per million). At the start of the 21st century, it is 0.035 percent (or 350 parts per million).

One of the main reasons for the increase in carbon dioxide in the atmosphere is deforestation, especially of the rain forests. Because of their high growth rate and biomass, rain forests play a large part in the carbon cycle. The trees take in huge amounts—about 22 billion tons (20 billion metric tons) per year—of carbon dioxide from the atmosphere as they photosynthesize.

Deforestation of the rain forest has a double effect on carbon dioxide levels. First, the felled trees no longer take in carbon dioxide from the air. Second, when any remaining wood is burned for fuel or, as in slash-and-burn farming, to clear the ground, much of the carbon in the wood is released into the atmosphere as carbon dioxide. In addition the carbon dioxide released from the soil also goes into the atmosphere instead of being taken up again by the trees. Slash-and-burn deforestation may add 2.2 billion tons (2 billion metric tons) of carbon dioxide to the atmosphere every year. The other major reason for the increase in carbon dioxide is the burning of fossil fuels (coal, oil, and gas) in power stations, for heating, and in car engines.

Global Temperature Changes

Changes in global temperatures are not a new thing. The temperature has been going up and down since life first appeared on the earth over 4 billion years ago. One hundred million years ago, during the Age of the Dinosaurs, the temperature was about 18°F (10°C) warmer than it is today. Tens of thousands of years ago, during several ice ages, the earth's temperature was much cooler than today.

IN FOCUS

Carbon Dioxide Proportions

The atmosphere contains about 770 billion tn. (700 billion metric tons) of carbon dioxide. The burning of fossil fuels adds between 5.5 and 6.6 billion tn. (5 and 6 billion metric tons) per year, and the burning of rain forest wood about 2.2 billion tn. (2 billion metric tons) per year. However, about half of this excess carbon dioxide is taken up by plants, mostly in the rain forests, probably by increasing growth rates. More is taken into the oceans. Overall, about 3.3 billion tn. (3 billion metric tons) of carbon dioxide are added to the atmosphere every year.

In the second half of the 20th century, ecologists and meteorologists debated whether the current global warming was just part of the natural cycle of changing

Reforestation in Sri Lanka. As these saplings grow, they will take in carbon dioxide from the atmosphere to build up their plant tissues.

temperatures or was being created by human activities. Most experts now accept that humans are to blame.

Evidence and Effects

The evidence for global warming comes from weather records. They show an increase in average global temperature of about 0.9°F (0.5°C) in the 20th century, and that eight of the hottest years in the twentieth century occurred in the 1990s.

The effects of global warming are already being seen. Satellite photographs of the polar ice caps show that the caps are slowly shrinking. Some areas of the world are seeing evidence of climate change, with variations in rainfall patterns and amounts, unusual heat waves in summer, or very cold or stormy winters.

Researchers have made differing predictions about future global warming and its effects. Estimated figures for temperature increases range from 2°F to 8°F (1°C to 4°C) by the end of the 21st century. This will lead to more climate change, which in turn will affect which plants can grow where on Earth. Global warming will also lead to a rise in sea levels as the polar ice caps melt. The rise could be between 1½ and 4 inches (4 and 10 cm) per decade.

Low–lying islands, such as the Maldives, may be submerged if global warming triggers a rise in sea levels.

Low-lying islands, such as Pacific atolls, and coastlines could become submerged.

Changing Policies

Even if deforestation were stopped now and no more fossil fuels were burned, the effects of global warming so far would be felt for many decades. Several world summits have been held where politicians have tried to agree to reduce their countries' emissions of greenhouse gases, but many countries have yet to take action.

Reforestation would reverse the effect of deforestation because trees would remove excess carbon dioxide from the atmosphere as they grow. Reforestation would be highly expensive, but the cost would be small compared to the costs of the future effects of global warming. Unfortunately, we would need to plant a rain forest the size of Australia to counteract the increasing greenhouse gases.

Check these out:
● **Biomass** ● **Carbon Cycle** ● **Climate and Weather** ● **Deforestation** ● **Human Interference** ● **Pollution** ● **Reforestation**

Gorilla

The gorilla is one of our closest relatives. Perhaps the most intelligent animal on Earth after humans, gorillas live in the tropical forests of central Africa. There are three types of gorillas: mountain gorillas, western lowland gorillas, and eastern lowland gorillas.

Gentle Giants

A large male gorilla may be almost 6 feet (1.8 m) tall and can weigh up to 400 pounds (180 kg), but females are smaller. Despite their large size, gorillas pose little threat to other animals. They feed on plants using their massive back teeth (molars) to grind the tough plant material. Leaves and stems contain little nourishment, so gorillas have to

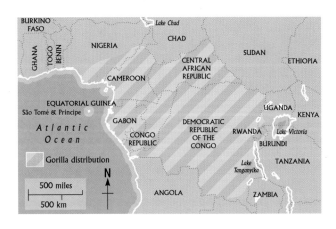

KEY FACTS

● **There are fewer than 250 mountain gorillas left.**

● **At night gorillas make nests of leaves and branches to sleep in. A nest may be a cushion on the ground or a platform in the fork of a tree.**

● **Individual gorillas can be recognized by their faces, especially the shape of their noses.**

spend a lot of their time eating. After a vigorous morning spent looking for food, the gorillas usually rest for an hour or two in the middle of the day.

Gorillas on the Go

In the lush tropical forests of Africa, food for gorillas is plentiful. Gorillas constantly move from one place to another. They do not completely strip the vegetation, giving it a chance to grow back.

Gorillas usually walk on all fours, resting their weight on the soles of their hind feet and on the knuckles of their hands. They can rear up on their hind legs, especially when angry or when challenged by a rival. Young gorillas are

The next generation—a mountain gorilla with her baby. Mountain gorillas are the most endangered gorillas of all.

A family of eastern lowland gorillas feeding. The huge silverback male is on the right.

good climbers and can swing from tree to tree by their arms. When they get older and heavier, they tend to stay on the ground.

Gorillas on the move leave trails of trampled vegetation, with knuckle prints on patches of bare earth and chains of droppings. The prints give a clue to the size of each animal. Gorillas may also leave behind evidence of their feeding— peelings from the stems of wild celery or thistle or strips of giant lobelia stems raked with tooth marks.

Unlike most plant-eating mammals, gorillas (especially the males) have large canine teeth (the sharp, pointed teeth behind the front teeth). Principally used in displays to intimidate attackers and other males and to impress females, males will also use these teeth in earnest to defend their mates and young.

Sociable Animals

Gorillas live in groups of 5 to 10 animals, sometimes as many as 20 or 30. Each group will have several females, various youngsters of different ages, and a single mature male.

A female gorilla can become pregnant at any time of year, but she usually produces only one baby every three to four years. A baby gorilla clings to its mother's belly at first, but once it is about four months old, it rides on its mother's back. When the young males approach adulthood, they set out on their own. They may pair up with lone females and form their own group. Young females may move around between groups.

Like human hair, the soft brownish black fur of a gorilla turns gray with age. Mature males are called silverbacks because they develop a silvery white saddle on their backs. Gorillas have bare pink faces when young, but their skin turns black as they grow older. When mature, males may fight a silverback for possession of his females.

Gorillas spend a lot of time grooming each other. Grooming helps keep their fur clean and reinforces the bond between male and female and between female and offspring. The females in a group that are not related to each other seldom groom each other.

Gorilla Conversations

Gorillas make at least 25 different sounds. The loudest is a hoot that can travel over a mile (1.6 km) through forest and is used by male silverbacks to challenge each other.

Gorillas scream to alert the group to danger. A less frightened gorilla may utter a high-pitched bark if it finds something it does not understand, and an irritated gorilla will grunt. Gorillas also croon, hum, purr, moan, wail, and howl.

Silverbacks have big chest muscles and hold them tight, like the skin of a drum. An angry silverback will roar and beat its chest with cupped hands, producing a hollow sound like a low-pitched drumming.

Gorillas in Danger

As Africa's human population grows, more and more forests are cut down and turned into farmland. In Rwanda, for example, there are already about 500 people living in every square mile (193 per km²) of countryside, and every year 27,000 new families need land for survival.

In some parts of Africa, gorilla flesh is considered a delicacy. Snares set for other animals also trap gorillas, which die a slow and painful death if not rescued. Some poachers steal young gorillas from reserves for the pet trade or for unscrupulous zoo owners, though baby gorillas seldom survive without their parents. Because the gorillas defend their young so fiercely, the poachers may have to kill up to 10 gorillas to take one baby.

Frequent civil wars plague many of the countries in which gorillas live, especially Rwanda and the Democratic Republic of the Congo. Millions of people take refuge in the forests, cutting down the trees for firewood and killing gorillas for meat. Rebels and guerrillas have made it impossible for forest rangers to work in some places, though many still risk their lives to try to protect the gorillas.

Gorillas cannot easily recover from such onslaughts. They produce only one young at a time, at intervals of about four years, and only about half the young survive.

Check these out:
- Africa
- Ape
- Communication
- Congo
- Endangered Species
- Mammal
- Poaching
- Primate

IN FOCUS

Gorilla Tourism

African governments have tried to help the gorillas by setting up special reserves, but they have little money to pay guards and rangers. The Rwandan government has sponsored awareness programs for schoolchildren and villagers and promoted the development of "gorilla tourism," protecting particular groups of gorillas and charging tourists high prices for supervised visits to see them. Villagers also sell the tourists locally made souvenirs, thus bringing money to the local economy and giving people another incentive to protect the gorillas.

Grasshoppers, crickets, and katydids all belong to the large order of insects called Orthoptera. This name means "straight wings," and it refers to the way the stiff front wings are folded straight back along the body. However, not all of these insects have well-developed wings; some have only a tiny flap on each side of their body, and some have no wings at all. Many of the fully winged species can fly, and some species can fly quite long distances.

KEY FACTS

● Grasshoppers' ears are on the sides of their body, while crickets and katydids have ears on their front legs.

● Many grasshoppers and katydids are so well camouflaged as leaves and twigs that predators miss them completely.

● Katydids got their name because people thought that the three-syllable calls of some species sounded like "Katy did."

These insects' most obvious feature is their long and muscular back legs, which enable them to make huge leaps. However, not all of them jump when they are disturbed. Grasshoppers usually leap away, while crickets are more likely to scuttle along on the ground, and katydids often just drop into the undergrowth.

Almost all grasshoppers are active in the daytime, while most crickets and katydids are nocturnal creatures. All of these insects possess powerful jaws, and many of the larger species will bite if they are handled.

All Orthoptera members start life as eggs, which are usually laid in holes in the ground or inside plants. The young insects, called nymphs, look like small versions of the adults, except that they have no wings at first; wings grow gradually on the outside of the body. Nymphs change their outer skins by molting several times as they grow into adulthood.

The raised spiky legs and wide-open jaws of this Amazonian katydid are likely to scare off most birds as well as other predators.

Insect Singers

Grasshoppers and other orthopteran insects are famous for the chirping songs males use to attract females. The sounds are produced by rubbing one part of the body against another in a process called stridulation. Grasshoppers rub their back legs against their front wings to make a noise, but crickets and katydids do it by rubbing their wings together. Each species has its own song, which attracts only the right kind of females.

The pitch of the song depends largely on the speed at which the legs or wings move; the greater the speed, the higher the pitch. Grasshoppers tend to make buzzing sounds with quite a low pitch, but crickets and katydids generally produce songs with a higher pitch. Ears for hearing the song differ in location depending on the species. Grasshopper ears are on the sides of their body, but crickets and katydids have ears on their front legs.

Grasshoppers

While most of the world's grasshopper species live in open grassy places, many have made their homes in the rain forests. They are almost entirely vegetarian. In response to the intense competition for food and living space, some of these rain forest species have adopted unusual habits, becoming quite unlike their grassland relatives. Some of them live on the ground and feed on dead leaves and fungi, and some even feed on animal droppings, which often contain undigested plant material. These ground-living species occur mainly in the gloomier parts of the forest; they are difficult to find because they so closely resemble dead leaves.

Most of the rain forest grasshoppers live in the lush vegetation of clearings and riverbanks. Mainly green or brown, they are usually well camouflaged, but some species go a good deal further. *Proscopia* species from South America are wingless and look amazingly like sticks, while species of *Chlorotypus* from Malaysia are almost indistinguishable from leaves. Some grasshoppers, including several weird-looking species from Madagascar, are protected by large spines along their bodies.

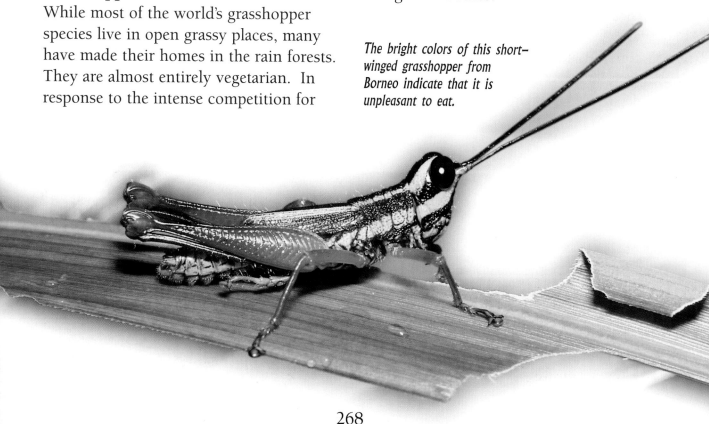

The bright colors of this short-winged grasshopper from Borneo indicate that it is unpleasant to eat.

Some rain forest grasshoppers are brightly colored, warning birds and other predators that they are poisonous. Grasshoppers of the *Zonoceros* species from tropical Africa are mainly yellow with red and black markings. Very conspicuous when sitting on a leaf, they are rarely attacked. Any bird that does molest one gets a beakful of foul-tasting foam pumped out from the insect's thorax.

Crickets

Crickets generally have a somewhat boxlike shape because their wings lay fairly flat on top of their body and then bend sharply downward at the sides. The female uses her needlelike ovipositor to lay her eggs in the soil. Most crickets are nocturnal, and some of them produce quite melodious, birdlike songs. Most crickets are omnivorous scavengers that live on the forest floor, although some prefer plant matter and some prefer to eat animal remains. *Brachytrupes membranaceus*, which is common in many parts of tropical Africa, is over 2 inches (5 cm) long and feeds on roots. It can destroy crops planted in and around the rain forest, though it is, in turn, eaten by local people.

Crickets are generally black or brown, although some tree-living species are brightly colored. *Rhicnogryllus lepidus* from eastern Africa, for example, is bright blue with black markings.

Forest Katydids

Katydids are usually quite slender insects. The wings, when present, are held vertically along the sides of the body, with just a small overlap near the front. The female has a bladelike ovipositor that is straight or curved and sometimes as long as the rest of her body. Species with long ovipositors usually push their eggs into the ground. Short and curved ovipositors usually have tiny teeth around the tip, used like little saws to cut slits in plants, where the eggs are then laid.

Katydids live mainly in trees and shrubs, and most of the rain forest species are some shade of green. They are primarily predatory creatures, eating a wide range of other insects, including grasshoppers and smaller katydids. However, some prefer to nibble leaves, and some are completely omnivorous.

IN FOCUS

The Lichen Katydid

The lichen katydid feeds on the tangled beard lichens (LIE-kuhns) in the dripping American rain forests. Its grayish green color, spiky legs, and pale wing veins blend totally with the surrounding lichens.

269

The strongly veined wings of this South American katydid look just like bright green leaves.

The insects sing mainly at night; the forest resounds with their songs. Some are shrill and squeaky, others are deep and throbbing; some are continuous, while others come in long or short bursts of sound repeated at regular intervals. The total effect can be quite deafening.

Perfect Camouflage

Katydids exhibit some of the animal world's most amazing examples of camouflage.

Their folded wings often have the shape and color of the surrounding leaves, and slender stripes on the wings are so similar to the veins in the leaves that even experienced naturalists cannot always pick out the insects. Their legs look like twigs and leaf stalks. *Zabalius apicalis* from tropical Africa has this form of camouflage, known as protective resemblance. Birds and other predators mistake the insects for leaves or twigs and take no further notice of them.

Most forest leaves tend to get a bit ragged after a while, and katydids have evolved features that copy this as well. Patches of brown on their wings and bodies look like the shriveled blotches on leaves that have been damaged by other insects or by fungi. The South American *Mimetica incisa* is a particularly good example of a katydid with this kind of camouflage.

IN FOCUS

Scaring Predators

Some katydids have large eyelike markings on their hind wings. Exposed only when the insects are alarmed, these markings resemble the eyes of cats or owls, and they scare off most small predators. Some katydids have transparent wings and show remarkable similarities to various wasps. Predators know that wasps can sting, so they leave the mimics alone as well.

Check these out:
● Camouflage ● Communication
● Insect ● Invertebrate

Herbs are plants whose fresh or dried leaves are used to add extra flavor to food. Most of them are harvested from herbaceous (nonwoody) plants. Spices are usually obtained from parts other than the leaves and are normally used in dried, powdered form. Herbs and spices are usually strongly scented, and most of them yield oils and perfumes as well.

Rain forests do not provide us with many herbs because herbaceous plants are not common there. Sweet basil, an essential ingredient of pesto, probably originated in or around the rain forests of tropical Asia, although it has been cultivated elsewhere for thousands of years. Lemongrass, which is used to flavor many Asian dishes, originally came from the edges of the forests of southern India and Sri Lanka.

KEY FACTS

● **Herbs and spices do not have much food value, but they can greatly improve the taste of other foods by adding subtle flavors.**

● **Herbs are usually fresh or dried leaves.**

● **Spices come from almost any part of a plant except the leaves and are usually used in powder form.**

Forest Spices

Many spices originated in the rain forests. Pepper is the world's most important spice; no other spice is used in such large quantities. For thousands of years it was used to disguise the flavor of bad meat (in the days before refrigerators) and is now used in all sorts of spicy dishes and sauces. Pepper comes from the small

Bunches of small tubular flowers are opening on this clove tree. To obtain the cloves, the flower buds must be harvested and dried before they open.

red fruits of a climbing plant that originally grew in the rain forests of Southeast Asia. Each fruit contains a large seed. The unripe fruits are dried to produce the black peppercorns ground in pepper mills. White pepper is obtained by crushing the seeds of ripe fruits after removing the outer skin.

IN FOCUS

Vanilla: The Sweetest Spice

Vanilla, used to flavor ice cream and a wide range of candies, cookies, and cakes, is obtained from the dried seedpods of an orchid. The plant originally came from tropical America but is now grown in many other tropical areas. Vanilla is extracted from the pods by dissolving it in various liquids; it is usually sold in the form of a solution or essence. The process is long and complicated and makes vanilla the world's second most expensive spice after saffron. Some vanilla is now made artificially, but this is not thought to be as good as the natural product.

Cinnamon, used to flavor cookies, cakes, and many other foods, comes from the bark of a small tree that originated in the forests of Sri Lanka and southern India. The bark is stripped from young trunks, and the outer bark is scraped away. The pale brown inner bark is then dried and sold in small strips or ground into powder.

Cloves are the dried flower buds of a small tree. They are used in apple pies and in some meat dishes, but one of the most popular uses is for flavoring mulled wine at Christmas. The clove tree is a native of Indonesia, and for a long time it was not grown anywhere else. Today most of the world's cloves are grown on the islands of Zanzibar and Madagascar.

Nutmeg comes from another Indonesian tree. The fruit, which looks like a peach, splits open when ripe to reveal a fleshy red network surrounding the large woody seed that is the actual nutmeg. The dried seed can be bought whole or in powdered form, on its own or as a component of mixed spice. It is often used for flavoring cakes and puddings. The red network around the seed produces a separate spice known as mace, which is generally used in savory dishes and sauces.

Ginger is obtained from rhizomes (RIE-zoems), which are underground plant stems, of a small bamboolike plant from the forests of tropical Asia. The dried rhizomes are ground up and used to flavor curries and many other dishes. Ginger is also used to give a slightly hot, spicy flavor to candies and cookies and to flavor ginger beer and ginger wine. Cooks also grate whole ginger rhizomes into food.

Check these out:
● Flowering Plant ● Food ● Fruit ● Orchid

Herbivores are animals that feed on plants. Plants offer animals many different kinds of food, from leaves, shoots, sap, fruits, and nuts to energy-rich nectar and protein-rich pollen.

Some herbivores, such as monkeys, eat most kinds of plant material, while others are specialists. Sloths feed only on leaves; hummingbirds, sunbirds, and honey possums feed on nectar; beetles nibble pollen; aphids and many other bugs suck sap; finches and barbets are seed eaters; while toucans and pigeons feed on fruits. All herbivores are prey for flesh-eating animals, the carnivores. In this way the nutrients stored in rain forest plants are passed up through the food chain.

KEY FACTS

● **The teeth of plant-eating mammals such as squirrels and deer keep growing throughout their lives to make up for the heavy wear caused by such a tough diet.**

● **The coconut crab of the Indian and Pacific Ocean coasts loves to feed on coconuts and will even climb coconut palms in search of dinner.**

● **Bees mix honey with saliva to make beebread, a food source for the colony.**

A Tough Meal

Plant stems and leaves are tough foods to tackle. Their cell walls contain cellulose, which most animals cannot digest, and leaves and stems also contain tough woody fibers. So animals need powerful teeth or jaws to chew the plant tissues into small pieces that are easier for the animals' digestive juices to work on.

Plant-eating mammals often have sharp front teeth (incisors) for biting off pieces of plants. A few herbivores, such as deer, have a horny pad instead of top teeth in front. Some have a gap, called a diastema (die-uh-STEE-muh), between the teeth that allows room for the tongue to mix the food thoroughly with saliva. Saliva contains digestive juices that soften and moisten the food.

Certain kinds of mammals called ruminants, such as deer, have a special chamber (rumen) in their stomach that contains bacteria and other microorganisms. After chewing their food, ruminants pass it into the rumen, and when it has been partly digested by the microorganisms,

A red colobus monkey feeding. Monkeys eat most kinds of plant material, using their hands to manipulate their food.

they regurgitate it and chew it some more. This breaks it down into even smaller pieces, producing a larger surface area that their own digestive juices can get to work on.

Termites feed on the toughest plant material of all—wood. Their stomachs contain a special chamber full of hundreds of different kinds of single-celled organisms too small to see without a microscope. These organisms can break down the tough plant fibers and cell walls, releasing nutrients that the termites can absorb.

Picking Leaves

Many herbivores use their muscular tongues to tear off leaves and shoots; elephants use their trunks. A few animals, like the tapirs (TAE-puhrs) and Indian rhinoceros, have long, muscular lips for twisting twigs till they break. Leaf-eating mammals have large back teeth (molars) with ridges for grinding the leaves; the upper and lower molars fit tightly together.

Caterpillars do not have teeth; instead, jagged edges, like little saws, line their hard jaws. Very few birds eat leaves, perhaps because birds have no teeth and tend to swallow their food whole.

Sap Suckers

Some animals tap directly into the veins that transport the food the plant is trying to consume—the sugars and other foods it makes by photosynthesis. Aphids (AE-fuhds) and other bugs have sharp, piercing mouthparts that drill into plant stems to reach the sap. The sap is under so much pressure inside the stem that it is literally pumped into the bug. Excess sugars ooze out of the other end of the bug and attract ants, which like to feed on them.

The sap inside the trunks of trees is harder to get at because bark surrounds it, but sapsuckers and other relatives of woodpeckers can drill deep enough to lap it up with their tongues. Marmosets, tamarins, and galagos use their teeth to scrape away the bark to get at the sap and gum below.

High-Energy Nectar

The sugary liquid produced by flowers is a rich source of energy, enough to support

RAIN FOREST HERBIVORES

Resplendent Quetzal

Asian Elephant

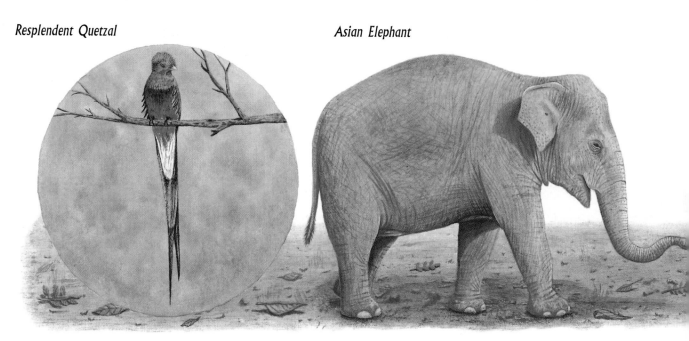

Underwater Herbivores

Some of the softest vegetation to chew includes water plants. Supported by water, they do not need a lot of woody fibers to hold them up. As well as fish such as carp, many mammals feed on underwater plants. Capybaras, large rodents that live along the banks of South American rivers and lakes, feed on the lush vegetation at the edge of the water.

the energetic lifestyle of the butterflies and birds that feed on it. Hummingbirds and some moths and bats hover in front of flowers as they suck up nectar with their long tongues. Hovering uses a lot of energy, and the nectar supplies it.

Butterflies, bees, mosquitoes, and other insects stand on the flower to feed. Bees have surprisingly long tongues, up to 1 inch (2.5 cm) long. Butterflies and moths have even longer tongues and can reach deep inside bell-shaped or tube-shaped flowers.

Their mouthparts form an extendable tube for sucking up the sweet liquid.

Pollen too is food for many animals, from beetles to bats. While nectar is rich in sugars, pollen contains a lot of protein. Female honeybees comb pollen from flowers with special hairs on their front legs, then scrape it into bristly baskets on their hind legs.

Feasting on Fruit
Fruits are important food for many mammals, birds, and insects. Wasps feed

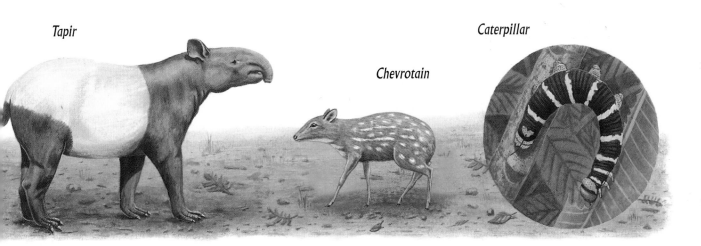

Tapir

Chevrotain

Caterpillar

on very ripe, juicy fruits. Monkeys, bats, bears, and many birds such as parrots, barbets, and toucans will flock to fruiting trees, while hogs, peccaries (which resemble pigs), and many smaller animals search for fallen fruits on the ground.

Plants use fruit-eating animals to disperse their seeds; the seeds are not digested, so they pass right through the animals and are shed in their droppings. Unripe fruits often contain poisonous or bitter-tasting chemicals to deter animals from eating them. Many fruits turn red, yellow, or orange as a sign that they are ripe to eat. In this way the animals eat the plant's fruits only when the seeds inside are mature enough to be dispersed.

Some birds feed on the seeds themselves. Finches have strong, sharp-edged beaks specially adapted for dealing with tough seed coats. The lower bill fits into a V-shaped cleft in the upper bill.

A honey possum feeds on a flower. Honey possums are specialists and depend upon a constant food source.

IN FOCUS

Safety in Numbers

Finches, barbets, and other small, seed-eating birds roam in large flocks through the forests searching for seeds and benefit from many pairs of eyes on the lookout for both food and predators. As many as 30 different species of birds may be found in a single flock.

Using its tongue, the finch places the seed in this cleft so that the joint in the seed coat is held against the sharp edge of the lower bill. Once it has cut through this part of the seed, the bird turns it around to crack on another part. Different bird species are adapted to handle different sizes of seeds.

A Nutty Problem

Nuts present even more of a challenge than seeds. Few birds have strong enough beaks to break open a nut, but some, such as finches, parrots, macaws, and cockatoos, can manage it. Parrots and cockatoos saw at nuts with their sharp beaks. Once they have made a hole in one, they slice at it with their hooked upper bills.

Pigs, peccaries, and forest hogs have powerful teeth and seem to favor nuts, but the masters of opening nuts are rodents—mice, rats, pacas, agoutis, and their relatives the squirrels. Their chisel-like front teeth can bore through the tough shell, and the teeth keep on growing throughout their lives, since the nuts wear them down.

Check these out:

Ant • Bat • Bee and Wasp • Bird • Butterfly and Moth • Deer • Ecosystem • Food Web • Fruit • Galago • Marmoset and Tamarin • Monkey • Pig and Peccary • Rodent • Seed • Squirrel • Termite

People have always used local materials to build their own homes. Two hundred years ago, pioneers in the United States felled pine trees to build log cabins. European peoples at that time built with stone, brick, slate, turf, or timber. In the Middle East, builders used mud bricks baked in the sun or reeds from the wetlands of Iraq. In eastern Africa they built homes from coral cement and mangrove poles.

KEY FACTS

● **Many rain forest buildings are raised on stilts, either to protect against flooding or against tropical snakes and insects.**

● **Up to 600 people may live in a single Dyak longhouse in the forests of central Borneo.**

Rain forest inhabitants were no exception. Living in remote areas and surrounded by dense forest, they had no choice but to use whatever building materials were close at hand. Fortunately rain forests offer a wide range of natural fibers and timbers that are practical to obtain and effective to use.

Timber, Thatch, and Vines

Most forest peoples around the world still build with the trunks and branches of local hardwood and softwood trees. Some tropical hardwood timbers are resistant to boring insects, and they do not rot as easily as softwoods. Oil palm fronds or bundles of other leaves are often used as thatch for the roofs. Tough vines can be used for lashing together beams and poles, binding thatch, and making rope bridges and ladders.

The Akha people live in China, Burma, Thailand, Laos, and Vietnam. They build a new village of bamboo and thatch every five years or so.

277

Fisherfolk build temporary shelters of leaves and branches on the banks of the Orinoco River in Venezuela. Their canoes are also made of rain forest materials.

Only in the last 100 years, as roads have been built and motorboats have traveled up tropical waterways, have other building materials such as corrugated iron sheeting or bricks been brought into rain forest regions. Such materials are not always suited to the local climate. Conditions in tropical rain forests are hot and humid, with high rainfall, and metals rust quickly.

Rain forest homes need to be cool and provide adequate shelter. Many traditional housing styles meet these needs perfectly, so they are still common in the world's rain forests today.

Housing the Community

The type of housing in which people live reflects their way of life. Bands of hunter-gatherers need to be on the move, so temporary shelters suit them well. Farmers too may move from one part of the forest to another, clearing patches of land that are then allowed to grow over once the soil has been exhausted. Their villages may be semipermanent.

People using more settled farming methods—growing cash crops on plantations or fishing—live in more permanent villages. These settlements may grow into towns, which gradually develop into major trade centers or river ports.

Rain forest communities have many different social structures. These may be based around families or clans, groups in which people share

IN FOCUS

Ruins and Creepers

Forests grow rapidly in hot and humid tropical climates. Once buildings have been abandoned, they are soon covered by creeping plants and vines. Advancing roots and heavy rainfall undermine buildings and make them collapse. Trees reclaim the clearings once made by people, and the forest returns. That is why it is often so hard for archaeologists to find any trace of ancient tropical civilizations. Sites such as the 900-year-old city of Angkor Wat in Cambodia, Southeast Asia, had to be hacked from dense layers of vegetation before they could be revealed to the modern world.

descent from a common ancestor. Men and women may have different roles, with only the men or only the women working the land. Some communities may have no leaders; others may have powerful chiefs or shamans. All these factors affect the various ways in which houses are built and villages are arranged in rain forest settlements around the world.

Many rain forests have cliffs where heavy tropical rainfall has carved out networks of caves. Caves have been used for shelter throughout human history, and some people still use them as homes.

Central African Camps

The peoples of the Central African rain forests, such as the Mbuti (em-BOO-tee) and the Baka (BAH-kah), build very simple shelters. Many of these hunter-gatherers make temporary forest camps that are inhabited for about six weeks at a time by groups of up to 40 people.

The small, domed shelters of the Mbuti people fill a clearing in the Democratic Republic of the Congo.

The men cut a clearing from the forest, but the women build the shelters. These may be rectangular lean-tos but more commonly are small, circular domes. To make the framework, the women bend and interlace saplings and then make an effective waterproof covering from overlapping large, glossy green leaves or palm fronds. Cooking takes place on campfires outside the house. Peoples like the Mbuti often spend part of the year camped near the permanent villages of farming peoples, to trade or work.

Western Africa Compounds

The Yoruba (YOE-roo-bah) people live primarily in the humid, tropical forest zone of southwestern Nigeria and southern Benin. Many are farmers, growing cash crops of oil palm and cocoa trees.

The traditional Yoruba dwelling place is a group of interconnected rectangular buildings extending around one main courtyard or compound and several smaller ones. Open to the sky, the courtyards provide both shade and fresh air. Pots in

the courtyard collect rainwater. The buildings' walls are of dried mud, and carved timber posts support the palm-thatched roofs. The various buildings may include men's quarters, women's quarters, workshops, and stores.

The Borneo Longhouse

Borneo is the largest island in Asia. Among its peoples are the Dyaks (DIE-aks), who make up about 200 different tribes. Most of the Dyaks live in the rain forests of the interior, with their villages built along riverbanks.

A Dyak tribe called the Iban (EE-bahn) farm temporary forest clearings and grow rice in swampy areas. Their homes, called longhouses, can stretch up to a quarter of a mile (0.4 km) long and house 600 people. These structures are raised above the ground on tall hardwood posts. The Iban reach a wooden platform not by stairs but by climbing notched logs. Some areas of the platform are open, while others support a series of rectangular family dwellings called *bilek* (BEE-lek). Many different families live in each longhouse as a single community, and boisterous children swarm everywhere. Each longhouse has a council of respected leaders and a chief.

In the past, having a whole community in a single raised longhouse made it easier to defend it from attacks by rival tribes of headhunters. Today, in more peaceful times, single-family dwellings often replace traditional longhouses.

The Yanomami Roundhouse

The Yanomami (ee-on-oe-MAH-mee) people live in the tropical rain forests of Brazil and Venezuela in South America. They hunt, fish, and grow crops such as bananas, plantains, sweet potatoes, and cassavas in forest clearings. Like the Iban of Borneo, many Yanomami families share the same home, which is well defended against raids by hostile local people or other intruders.

The Yanomami dwelling place is called a *shabono* (shah-BOE-noe). This large, circular structure is home to approximately 100 people. Poles support the palm-thatched roof, and a simple loosely bound outer wall of staves lets in the daylight. Inside the shelter, beaten earth provides a floor.

IN FOCUS

Modern Architecture

There is a growing demand for eco-tourism, visits to the rain forest that do not damage its fragile environment. This has led to buildings being raised that are ultramodern in their design but that fit in with the rain forest in much the same way as traditional forest homes.

The outer rim of the *shabono* is divided into family areas. The air is smoky, for each family has its own hearth for cooking. People sleep on hammocks slung between the poles. The central area is communal and is used for meetings and important rituals such as dancing.

The Big Cone

A people called the Piaroa (pee-ah-ROE-ah), known by various other names, live in the far south of Venezuela, on the southern banks of the Orinoco River. Their way of life is similar to that of the Yanomami, and they too share their living quarters.

Their shelter, however, follows a different design. It is called a *churuata* (chew-RAH-tah) and can be over 30 feet (9 m) high. Its broad, circular base rises as a dome, but this narrows to a tall, slender cone at the top. It is entered through a rectangular door. The whole structure is thatched with a thick, shaggy layer of palm fronds.

Owning Homes and Land

Many rain forest communities are remote from cities and centers of political power. Many are denied formal ownership of land on which they and their ancestors have lived and built their homes for hundreds of years.

To some indigenous peoples, the whole idea of land ownership and property seems strange. The forest, they believe, is the creation of God or a spirit and cannot be owned. However, title to the land (legal ownership) is crucial to the survival of many rain forest peoples. It means they can control the way they settle and live on the land.

Check these out:

- Ashaninka People
- Dyak People
- Hunter-Gatherer
- Ibo People
- Kaluli People
- Kayapo People
- Kuna People
- Makah People
- Maya People
- Mbuti People
- Miskito People
- People of the Rain Forest
- Quinault People
- Resettlement
- Tlingit People
- Yanomami People

A churuata *is being built by Piaroa villagers in the rain forest of southern Venezuela. The framework of branches is in the process of being thatched.*

All living creatures interact with their environment. They have no choice. They are all part of the same web of life, the same global ecosystem. However, we humans tend to actively interfere with the world in which we live.

This characteristic has been the secret of our success. However, human interference is destroying many of the planet's most precious resources, including the world's tropical rain forests. In the last 100 years, human activity has turned vast areas of rain forest into barren wastelands and driven animals and plants to extinction.

KEY FACTS

● **Commercial logging and clearing forests by burning accounts for about 8 percent of all the human-produced gases that pollute the earth's atmosphere and cause the global climate to become warmer.**

● **The magnificent monkey-eating eagle is one of the world's biggest eagles—and one of the rarest. People have cleared its forest hunting grounds and killed the bird or collected it for zoos and museums.**

Greed for Resources

People take and make use of the many resources that the rain forest has to offer. They fell its trees, they saw the timber for building and furniture making, and they pulp it to make paper. Local peoples also use wood as fuel for cooking fires and for making charcoal.

Some people capture or kill the animals that live in the rain forest, taking parrots for illegal sale to collectors and selling meat, hides, and ivory elephant tusks. In times of hardship, they may kill large numbers of wild animals for food.

Farmers want the forest for its land. They burn off large areas to make room for grazing or crops. At first the land gives good yields, but it is quickly exhausted, and tropical rains often wash away the soil.

Prospectors search the forest for minerals beneath the ground. Gold is mined in the Amazon River basin in South America, and oil is extracted from the densely forested Niger River delta in western Africa.

Loggers, farmers, poachers, and miners all

Swaths of forest have been cleared to make room for tourist accommodation in peninsular Malaysia.

IN FOCUS

Spoiled by Oil

Nigeria is the 12th largest oil producer in the world, and oil accounts for over 90 percent of its exports. The country's large population depends on oil wealth for its survival. However, the impact of the international oil companies has been severe for the environment and also for the local peoples. Pollution levels there are far higher than those that European or North American governments would permit. Oil flares coat the landscape in black soot. Oil spills from broken pipelines (below) and leaks from waste pits have poisoned rivers and wetlands. Fish have died, and the surrounding land has been made barren. Local peoples such as the Ogoni have protested that while they suffer the effects of such dangerous exploitation of the natural environment, they have received little in compensation, since the wealth has not been returned to the local community.

open up the forest to the outside world. New roads, airstrips, and pipelines are built. Rivers become polluted. Towns sprawl across the landscape, preventing the free movement of wild animals.

Doing the Right Thing

Of course, not all human interference is destructive. Most indigenous hunters and gatherers learned long ago to use the world's rain forests without harming them. Long-standing tropical farming methods allow for temporarily clearing land, which is then allowed to grow over and recover.

In recent years many other people have interfered in the rain forests—but for the right reasons. Their aim is to safeguard the future of this precious global resource. They have carried out scientific research into the huge variety of rain forest plants and animals, discovering that many forest plants provide valuable medicines. They have campaigned for new laws to protect wildlife and plants and have created new reserves and protection areas. They have tried to manage forests so that they are sustainable, able to be renewed. They have supported the land rights of native, or indigenous, peoples living in the rain forests and tried to help them survive and adapt to the economic forces of the modern world. For example, in some areas indigenous peoples gather rain forest plants, nuts, and fruits that provide the raw materials for soaps, shampoos, medicines, and foods sold worldwide; this, in turn, provides them with an income without harming the rain forest.

Check these out:

- Cattle Ranching
- Clear-Cutting
- Exploitation
- Forestry
- Logging
- Mining
- Oil Exploration
- Pollution

Humidity

In the summer in North America, the weather often feels sticky as well as hot. This is because the air contains a lot of water vapor. It is said to be humid.

The air in the Tropics is normally very humid. This moisture in the atmosphere helps create heavy rain in the rain forest and is vital for the growth and decay of rain forest plants.

Water Vapor

Evaporation happens when water molecules escape from the surface of a body of water. It occurs when water boils, but it can also happen at temperatures lower than water's boiling point. For example, puddles gradually dry up as their water evaporates. The opposite of evaporation is condensation, which happens when water vapor cools and turns back into liquid.

Air can hold only a certain amount of water vapor before it becomes saturated. The higher the air temperature, the more water vapor it can hold before saturation is reached. Thus, warm air can be more humid than cold air.

If humid air is cooled, it eventually reaches the temperature at which it is saturated; this is called its dew point. If the air is cooled any more, it cannot hold all the water vapor, and some condenses to form water droplets. This is what happens when warm, humid air is breathed onto a cold mirror.

Measuring Humidity

Humidity is the amount of water vapor in the air. There are two different measurements of humidity: absolute and relative. Absolute humidity is the amount of water vapor in a certain volume of air. Relative humidity is the more common measurement. It is the amount of water vapor in the air as a percentage of water vapor the same air could possibly hold. Extremely dry air has a relative humidity of 0 percent; saturated air has a relative humidity of 100 percent. Humidity is measured with an instrument called a hygrometer.

IN FOCUS

How Humans Adapt to Heat

Humans are cooled by sweating. The evaporation of sweat takes heat away from the skin. However, when the air is very humid, evaporation is matched by condensation, which is why we feel sweaty. After thousands of years of living in rain forests, the indigenous peoples have become well adapted to these conditions. Their bodies work more slowly than other people's (for example, their hearts beat more slowly), which means they create less heat. They also have almost no body hair that would retain heat.

Rain Forest Humidity

The relative humidity of tropical air is normally very high, between about 75 and 90 percent. Under the rain forest canopy on the forest floor, it is an amazing 95 percent most of the time. This warm, moist microclimate is perfect for the growth of delicate plants such as orchids, and also for decomposers such as fungi that help recycle rain forest nutrients.

Water vapor is an important part of the water cycle and is responsible for the high rainfall in the rain forests. Plants give off water vapor through their leaves in a process called transpiration. Rainwater also evaporates from leaves. Water vapor from both sources rises into the air and condenses to form clouds. More than three-quarters of it falls again as rain, helping to

Morning mist over rain forest in Malaysia. Mist forms when humid air over the forest cools as the temperature drops at night.

recycle nutrients. In other biomes (large geographic regions made up of distinctive plant and animal communities), more than three-quarters of water vapor comes from evaporation over seas and oceans.

Deforestation drastically reduces the amount of water vapor that returns to the air from the area of cleared forest. The clearing of an entire rain forest would have a severe effect on the climate of the area by reducing rainfall. In turn this would reduce the chance of the forest regenerating.

Check these out:
● Climate and Weather ● Season ● Water

Hummingbird

Hummingbirds belong to a family of birds called the Trochilidae. There are more than 300 known species; the majority of these are found in the forests of Central and South America. The hummingbird family includes the world's smallest birds, which lay the smallest birds' eggs in the world's smallest birds' nests.

The largest species of hummingbird, the giant hummingbird, reaches nearly 8 inches (20 cm) in length, while the smallest, the tiny bee hummingbird, measures about 1 inch (2.5 cm), weighs under 0.07 ounce (2 g) and has the title of the world's smallest bird. The hummingbird family also includes some of the most brightly colored birds in the world.

Hummingbirds are active during the day. They are specialist nectar feeders, with long, thin beaks and even longer tongues to get deep inside flowers to reach the stores of nectar hidden there. The hummingbird feeds by hovering in front of a flower while its wings beat at a rate of up to 70 beats a second, just a blur to the human eye.

A Hummingbird's Flight

The hummingbird hovers with its body in an almost vertical position, so instead of beating up and down, its wings beat backward and forward in a sort of figure-eight movement. This means the bird gets lift from both the forward and backward strokes of the wingbeat, enabling it to hover. One or two

KEY FACTS

● The world's smallest bird is the tiny bee hummingbird, the size of a bumblebee.

● Hummingbirds are the only birds that can fly backward.

● A hummingbird uses up 150,000 calories a day, compared to our own average of 3,500 calories.

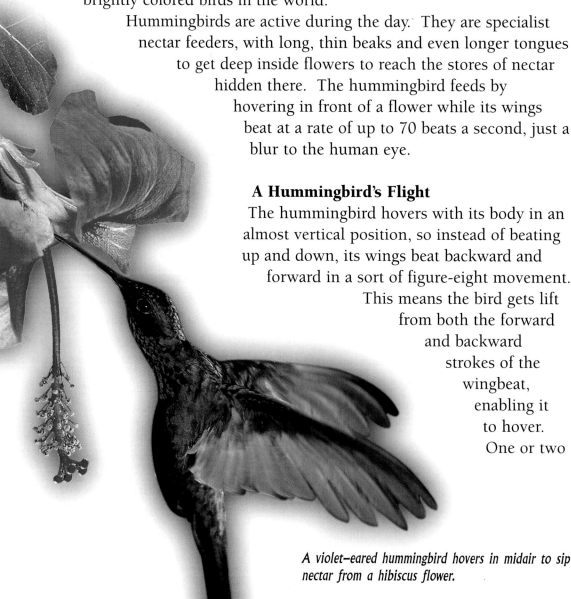

A violet-eared hummingbird hovers in midair to sip nectar from a hibiscus flower.

rain forests of Central America. These snakes often coil up inside heliconia flowers, which are the same color as they are, and wait for a hummingbird to come and feed. They then strike and kill it with their deadly poison.

Mating on the Wing

Outside the breeding season, hummingbirds are solitary, and males defend their territory vigorously. During the mating season, the male displays to the female by flying around in an arc and singing to her. Mating takes place in the air. Their tiny nest, which is not much bigger than an eggcup, is made of moss, lichen (LIE-kuhn), and spider's web silk; it is normally built in the fork of a small twig. The female lays two tiny eggs that hatch after 18 to 21 days. The chicks grow quickly on a diet of nectar (supplemented by small insects in some species). They fledge, growing adult feathers and leaving their nest, when three weeks old.

Check these out:
● **Bird** ● **Flowering Plant** ● **Nest and Nest Building** ● **Pollination**

other species of birds have the ability to hover but with nowhere near the skill exhibited by the hummingbirds. Being so active means that the hummingbird burns lots of calories, often as much as 150,000 a day compared to our own average of 3,500 calories. To supply its energy needs, the bird must visit well over a thousand flowers a day for their nectar.

The hummingbird's flight is also highly maneuverable; it can move backward and forward into flowers. In fact, hummingbirds are the only birds that can fly backward.

Keeping Out of Danger

This high degree of maneuverability also prevents the hummingbird from being caught by predators. Birds of prey find it difficult to dive and snatch under the rain forest canopy, and predatory mammals such as small cats are simply too slow for the hummingbird. However, there is one animal that occasionally manages to catch one. The eyelash viper is a small venomous snake found throughout the

IN FOCUS

A Brilliant Hummingbird

The ruby-topaz hummingbird lives in the rain forests of tropical South America from Colombia down to Chile. It is one of the smaller members of the family, with a length of 3½ in. (9 cm), and one of the more brilliantly colored, with an iridescent ruby head and golden chest.

Hunting and gathering is the oldest way of life known to humans. Wandering through the world, finding things to eat, sleeping in simple shelters, hunter-gatherers live as our oldest ancestors did. However, few such groups of people are left today. Those that survive live mainly in South America and Africa, with smaller groups still existing in India, Sumatra, Malaysia, and the Philippines.

Although groups of hunter-gatherers differ in small details, in general their way of life is similar around the world. Typically men and growing boys are the hunters while the women and young children are the gatherers. They have learned through generations of experience what is good and safe to eat.

KEY FACTS

● **In rain forests the lack of seasons means that hunter-gatherers can find food all year round.**

● **The blowguns used by Dyak hunters can be as long as 23 ft. (7 m).**

A Hunter's Weapons

The most common way of hunting in the rain forest, as elsewhere, is by using traps and snares, but sometimes other weapons are more successful. In thick forest there is no need for long-range weapons; small bows and arrows are enough. The Asmat (AHZ-maht), who live in Irian Jaya, New Guinea, are accurate archers, but the range of their weapons is less than 33 feet (10 m).

In the rain forests of the Congo River, the Aka (AH-ka) use arrows tipped with poisons made from plants to kill small animals. Many of the hunter-gatherers in South and Central America also use poison, sometimes curare (made from a vine) and sometimes the venom produced by poison dart frogs. They catch the frogs and suspend them over a fire. The frog then produces a deadly poison from glands in its skin. The hunters collect the poison in a small dish and smear the tips of their arrows with it.

The Dyak (DIE-ak) people of Borneo use a unique weapon, the blowgun. A long stem of bamboo is found; its woody central divisions inside are

Boys learn hunting skills from their fathers. These members of the Mbuti people live in western Africa.

288

Hunter–gatherers respect and honor the forest plants that provide their food. Here in the Asmat region of Irian Jaya, men perform a ceremony in honor of the sago palm.

move through the forest, the people collect leaves, roots, crabs, frogs, and even spiders.

The Semang (suh-MANG) in Malaysia, of whom less than 4,000 survive, hunt with blowguns and gather roots and fruits. Traveling around the forest in extended family groups, they shelter under rocky overhangs, making windbreaks out of forest leaves.

American Hunter-Gatherers
Most of the South American hunter-gatherers have died out. Among the survivors are the Guahibo (gwah-HEE-boe) and the Chiricoa (cheer-ee-KOE-ah), about 20,000 of whom live in Colombia and Venezuela. Their main quarry is the armadillo, though they are also successful fisherfolk. The Warrau (wah-RAH-ow) hunter-gatherers also live in Venezuela, along the Orinoco River delta, where they catch fish as well as hunt in the forests.

punched out and the interior is polished. A dart, often poisoned with the sap of the upas (YOO-puhs) tree, is then put into the lower end of the tube. With one puff, the hunter blows the dart out. With this weapon the Dyak can kill birds high above them in the trees. The largest blowguns are as long as 23 feet (7 m).

Asian Hunter-Gatherers
The Asmat people still follow their ancient forest way of life. Every week the whole village goes out to fell a sago (SAE-goe) palm. The sago provides the Asmat with their staple diet. The men fell the tree, then the women soak its fleshy inner pulp and squeeze out the starch. One day's work feeds four families for a week. In fallen dead trees, they can find palm beetle grubs that provide them with protein and fat. Megapode eggs, laid by a bird that nests in a mound of soil on the forest floor, are a welcome bonus. When the Asmats return home, the food is shared equally among all the members of the village. As they

Check these out:
- Dyak People ● Homes in the Rain Forest
- Mbuti People ● People of the Rain Forest

IN FOCUS
A Palm of Plenty
Like many other forest peoples, the Warrau have discovered a wild palm called moriche (moe-REE-chay), that can supply many of their needs. They make the pith of the palm into bread, eat its fruit, and make their clothes and hammocks from its fibers. They also brew its sap into an alcoholic drink.

Hydroelectricity is electricity generated by harnessing the energy in flowing water. It is produced at hydroelectric power stations, which are supplied with water constantly flowing through a dam. The larger the river, the more hydroelectricity the power station can produce.

Because rain forests grow in areas of the world where rainfall is high all year round, they are also in areas where large river systems offer huge potential for producing hydroelectricity. The Amazon River system could provide as much electricity from hydroelectric power stations as dozens of coal-fired power stations.

Today's rain forests are in countries where industries are being developed and populations are growing quickly, so new supplies of electricity are needed. The obvious answer is to build enormous "super dams" to provide cheap electricity without the problems of pollution from coal-fired stations or nuclear waste from atomic power plants.

Making Hydroelectricity

At most large hydroelectric power stations, water is stored in a reservoir behind a large dam. This provides a constant supply of water for the power station as the river flow changes. The water flows through turbines that turn generators, producing electricity. Large dams can be more than 1,000 feet (300 m) high, with power stations that create tens of gigawatts of electricity (one gigawatt is enough to light 10 million lightbulbs).

Although the main reason for building a large dam is to generate electricity, dams also have other benefits. They supply water for industries, homes, and

Rain forest trees drowned under Kenyir Lake, the reservoir formed behind Malaysia's largest hydroelectric dam.

Dams under Scrutiny

An amazing 20 percent of the world's freshwater flows through the Amazon River basin, so it is no surprise that 90 percent of Brazil's electricity comes from hydroelectric power stations. Brazil's first Amazonian super dam was the Tucuruí Dam (below), completed in the mid-1980s. It provides electricity for Brazil's huge metal-extracting industry. However, it submerged 676 sq. mi. (1,750 km²) of rain forest and displaced 40,000 people. Brazil has a huge dam-building program that includes more than 20 super dams in the Amazon River basin. It has been strongly criticized, and local protests have led international funding to be withdrawn.

farmland irrigation. They also help prevent flooding by catching floodwater and releasing it slowly downstream. Large reservoirs can also support fishing.

Dam Problems

Unfortunately, large dams create as many problems as they solve. Huge areas of land are drowned under the reservoir. This means that rain forest is lost, along with animals' habitats, and many people are forced from their homes, farms, and hunting land.

Dams upset the ecology of the river they impede. Fish and other animals can no longer move up and down the river. Algae often grow in the reservoir, choking off other forms of life. Downstream from the dam, the floodplains along the river no longer receive the annual flooding that

brings nutritious silt. This affects plants, animals, and farmers. Stagnant water at the edges of the reservoirs becomes a breeding ground for disease-spreading creatures such as mosquitoes. Some scientists believe that the methane gas produced by decaying plants drowned by reservoirs could have a greater impact on global warming than would coal-fired power stations of equal electricity output.

Several large dam projects have been canceled because of local and international protests, but many more are going ahead, without complete evaluation and planning, according to environmental groups.

Check these out:

● **Exploitation** ● **Human Interference**
● **River** ● **Water** ● **Watershed**

Ibo People

The land between the Niger and Cross Rivers in southeastern Nigeria supports a belt of dense rain forest. This is the homeland of the Ibo (EE-boe) people (also known as the Igbo), as well as of several smaller ethnic groups. Some Ibo also live northeast of the rain forest zone.

The Ibo number about 17 million. They are part of the larger ethnic grouping known as Bantu, and their language belongs to the Kwa family, within the Niger-Congo language group.

From Forests to Cities

The Ibo probably originated in the area where the Benue River meets the Niger and moved southeast over 4,000 years ago. They are closely related to the Yoruba (YOE-roo-bah) and other neighboring peoples. They suffered at the hands of European slave traders in the 1700s; many captives were shipped across the Atlantic Ocean. Today many African-Americans and Afro-Caribbeans are of Ibo descent.

The Ibo were farmers who cleared land by slashing and burning the forest before developing more settled farming methods. Today many have moved on to live in big cities and in many other regions of Nigeria, working in the oil

KEY FACTS

● **There are 17 million Ibo people.**

● **The Ibo have a traditional faith in a God who created the world, in an Earth Goddess, and in many spirits. Today, however, most Ibo are Christian, members of the Roman Catholic Church.**

Drumming and dancing are an important part of everyday life in Ibo communities.

292

IN FOCUS

Forest Fare

What might you find in an Ibo kitchen? Soups made from plantains (cooking bananas), corn, and chili; or peanuts, yams, and okra; deep-fried balls of mashed yams, chicken, and rice; and stews of beans, vegetables, and pumpkin.

industry of the Niger River delta, in commerce, government, construction, and education.

Even so, the Ibo still keep in touch with the villages they originally came from. In the past the Ibo have clashed with other Nigerian peoples, and in the late 1960s they tried to break away to form their own country, which they called Biafra (bee-AH-fruh). After a terrible civil war, they were defeated.

Tropical Farming

The majority of Ibo still farm plots of land in the rain forest belt, growing tropical crops. Palm oil is an important cash crop, grown for export, but most other crops are grown for their own use. Any surplus is sent to the open-air market of the district, which is the focus of social life. There, villagers haggle over the price of bananas or peanuts. They clamber aboard crowded trucks and minibuses, many of them painted with religious slogans or proverbs, to return home.

Varieties of crops are alternately grown on each piece of land, and this prevents the soil from becoming exhausted or eroded. Men grow mainly yams, while the women are responsible for growing other crops such as melons, okra, pumpkins, beans, and cassava. The women are also the chief market traders.

Ibo Way of Life

An Ibo village is surrounded by a wall, and the dwellings are made up of compounds (adjoining buildings set around a series of courtyards). A single household takes in an extended family—the male householder, his wife, their children, brothers, sisters, and elderly relatives. Property is passed down from father to son. Ancestors are traditionally honored at special shrines, usually with religious statues carved from forest hardwoods. These are fine examples of Ibo art.

Most Ibo men wear Western dress, but their traditional outfit is a tunic. The women often wear cotton dresses or long, brightly colored cotton wraps, with scarves tied into a turban.

Check these out:
- Africa
- Homes in the Rain Forest
- Mbuti People
- People of the Rain Forest

These Ibo youngsters still live in the forested countryside of their southeast Nigerian homeland.

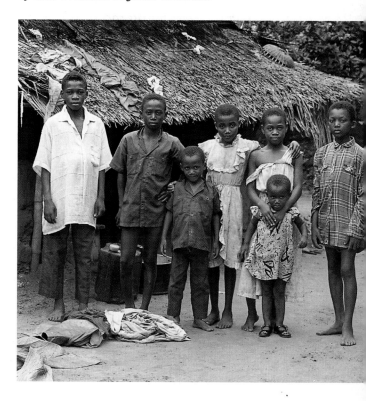

Iguanas are large lizards. Nearly all of them live in the warmer parts of the Americas. About 650 different species of lizards belong to the iguana family, although only the largest members are called iguanas.

Iguanas are found mainly in North and South America and the Caribbean, with a few on the islands of Madagascar, Fiji, Tonga, and the Galápagos. They include the anoles of Central and South America, with their brightly colored throat flaps (dewlaps); the helmeted lizard of South America, which has a bony helmet and a tall crest that can be erected for display; the casque-headed lizard; and the long-legged lizards, slow-moving nocturnal tree dwellers that lie in wait for prey.

KEY FACTS

● **Iguanas can be distinguished from most other lizards by their spiky crests and inflatable "beards," or skin flaps.**

● **Iguanas also have longer legs than most other lizards, enabling them to run at high speeds.**

● **Smaller iguanas feed mainly or entirely on insects and other animals, but the big ones are vegetarians.**

The Green Iguana

The green iguana is one of the best-known species in the rain forests of Central and South America. It is also known as the common iguana, and this is probably a better name because it is often brown, not green. This lizard is up to 6½ feet (2 m) long, although the tail makes up more than half of this length. Like most other iguanas, a spiky crest runs all the way along its back. It raises the spikes when it is angry or afraid, and it also inflates a large skin flap under its throat. This makes it look rather fierce, but it is really quite timid and shy.

The green iguana is an excellent climber and spends much of its time in the trees; it is surprisingly nimble for such a large animal.

A common iguana rests on a floating log. Its reptilian skin and characteristic spiky crest are clearly visible.

The Basilisk

South America's basilisk (BA-suh-lisk) is a relatively small member of the iguana family, about 2 ft. (60 cm) long and living in trees and bushes around the edges of lakes and rivers. The basilisk feeds on a variety of plants and insects. It swims well but is best known for its ability to run across the water when alarmed. Its back legs are much longer than its front ones, and it has long, fringed toes. As long as the basilisk is moving fairly quickly, the toes spread its weight, and it can run over the water in a semierect position without sinking. Some Native Americans call it the Jesus Christ lizard for this reason. It can also run over the ground and along branches in this posture, with its tail held out behind to balance it.

If it does miss its footing, it can fall 50 feet (15 m) or so without harm. However, it is more likely to fall into the water, for it likes to live in trees close to rivers. It can swim well by waving its tail from side to side.

Like the other large iguanas, the green iguana is mainly vegetarian. Youngsters eat a lot of insects, but as they grow up, they turn more and more to plants. Flowers and fruits are their main foods, together with some leaves and buds.

The female lays up to 70 round white eggs in a burrow up to 6 feet (1.8 m) long and up to 3 feet (1 m) below the surface. The eggs are similar in size to golf balls, and they hatch in about three months. The young iguanas are about 5 inches (12 cm) long when they hatch, and they grow quickly. They can grow to more

than 3 feet (1 m) in length before they are a year old.

Many Enemies
Although iguanas are well camouflaged in trees, they still have numerous enemies. Hawks and eagles snatch them from the treetops, while snakes take basking lizards by surprise. Iguanas are not safe on the ground either, falling prey to jaguars, other cats, and caimans. However, people are probably the greatest enemies of the green iguana. Its forest home is being destroyed, and people also hunt it for food. Its flesh is said to taste like chicken.

Check these out:
- Central America
- Chameleon
- Gecko
- Lizard
- Reptile

Glossary

Anthropologist: a scientist that studies human societies, past and present.

Aquatic: an animal or plant that lives in water.

Biomass: a measure of the amount of living matter (both animals and plants) in a certain area.

Biome: a large area that is distinguished by its climate and vegetation. Tropical rain forest is one type of biome, desert is another kind of biome.

Brachiation: when an animal propels itself through the trees by swinging its arms.

Caecilian: a long, thin, legless amphibian that at first glance resembles a large earthworm.

Carbohydrate: any of a wide range of substances consisting entirely of carbon, hydrogen, and oxygen. Glucose is one of the simplest carbohydrates. Energy-rich foods such as cane sugar, sucrose, and starch have a more complex structure than glucose. Cellulose, which is a plant's main building material, is a complex carbohydrate.

Chlorofluorocarbon: a greenhouse gas that contains chlorine, fluorine, and carbon.

Chlorophyll: the green substance inside a plant that converts sunlight into energy.

Corrugated iron: sheet metal formed into ridges for strength; used as a building material.

Diurnal: active during the day (as opposed to *nocturnal* which means active during the night).

Emissions: gases released into the atmosphere when fossil fuels are burned in power plants or in engines.

Fledge: the stage when a young bird is able to fly and is therefore ready to leave the nest.

Floodplain: a flat area on either side of a river onto which the river floods during periods of heavy rain.

Fossil fuel: a fuel made deep underground over millions of years from the remains of ancient animals and plants. Oil, coal, and natural gas are fossil fuels.

Fruiting body: that part of a fungus that is normally produced above ground for the purpose of producing spores. What we call mushrooms and toadstools are fungal fruiting bodies.

Guerrilla: a member of a small fighting force that moves about an area attacking conventional military forces and carrying out acts of sabotage and terrorism.

Hardwood timber: timber from slow-growing deciduous trees, whose close grain makes it ideal for furniture and carving.

Humus: decaying plant matter.

Indigenous: native, belonging to the region or district.

Infrared: a type of heat radiation that comes from hot objects. It is how heat reaches the earth from the sun and what you feel when the sun's rays warm your face.

Leach: when a liquid percolates through material.

Metamorphosis: a process in which an animal makes a complete change in its shape, appearance, and behavior as it grows to adulthood, i.e., from a tadpole to a frog or a caterpillar into a butterfly.

Microorganism: an organism (living creature) too small to see without the aid of a microscope.

Nectary: a patch of cells in a plant that secrete the sweet, sugary liquid known as nectar. Nectaries usually occur in the flowers, often at the bases of the petals, but also occur on the leaves and stems of some plants.

Nocturnal: active during the night.

Nutrient: a substance that a plant or animal needs to take in from its surroundings in order to live and grow. Nutrients provide energy and vital components for cells and tissues.

Omnivorous: an animal that eats both meat and vegetable matter.

Ovipositor: the egg-laying part of a female insect.

Photosynthesis: the building up of chemical compounds using light energy.

Primate: an animal of the family of apes and monkeys, including humans.

Pulp: wood that has been treated so that its fibers separate out; used to make paper.

Regurgitate: to bring partly-digested food from the stomach back up into the mouth (for re-chewing).

Respiration: the process by which animals and plants take in oxygen and use it to turn sugars into energy for movement and growth. A by-product of animal respiration is carbon dioxide.

Scavenger: a creature that feeds mainly on dead plants and animals.

Silt: a substance made of very tiny particles of rock deposited on river and sea beds by flowing water.

Slash-and-burn farming: farming that takes place on land cleared by cutting down and burning rain forests.

Spore: a minute, dustlike reproductive cell produced by mosses, liverworts, ferns, and fungi.

Terrestrial: an animal or plant that lives on land.

Thorax: the part of the body between the neck and abdomen of an invertebrate.

Transpiration: to lose water by evaporation.

Vertebrate: an animal that possesses a backbone or vertebrae.

Index

Numbers in *italics* indicate photographs.

agoutis 240
algae 252, 291
Amazon river 290–291
Angkor Wat 278
Aka people 288
Akha people 277
ants 241, 274
    army or driver 241
    leaf–cutter 252–253
aphids 274
Asmat people 289, *289*

bacteria 240, 273
Baka people 279
bats 275–276
bears 276
bees and wasps 275–276
beetles 240–241, 273, 275
    dung 241, *241*
birds 240, 274
    barbets 273, 276
    cockatoos 276
    eagle
      monkey–eating 282
    finches 273, 276
    hummingbirds 273, 275,
      286–287

bee 286
    giant 286
    ruby–topaz 287
    stripe–tailed 287
    violet–eared *286*
    jewel thrushes 241
    macaws 241, 276
    parrots 241, 276
    pigeons 273
    pittas 241
    resplendent quetzal 251, *274*
    sunbirds 273
    toucans 273, 276
Brazil 291
bush babies (SEE Galagos)
butterflies and moths 275

camouflage 270
capybaras 275
carbon cycle 261–263
caterpillars 274, *275*
centipedes 241
chevrotains 275
Chiricoa people 289
clear–cutting 242
climate 284–285
cockroaches 240
conservation 242, 283
crab, coconut 273

crickets 267–270
    brachytrupes
      membranaceus 269
    rhicnogryllus lepidus 269

dams 290–291
    Turucui dam *291*
decomposers 252, 285
deer 273
deforestation 238–239,
    260–263, 285
Dyak people 280, 288–289

elephants 274, *274*
erosion 242

farming 244–245, 262,
    282–283, 292–293
ferns 240
figs 251
food chain 273
forest fires 238–239,
    238–239, 243
forest floor 240–241, *240*,
    244, 253
forestry 242–245
    agroforestry 244–245, *244*
    artificial regeneration 244
    natural regeneration
      243–244
    seed orchards 245

selective felling 242–243
frogs and toads 246–249
    camouflage 249
    poisonous 246–247, 249
    reproduction 247–249
    species of frog:
        goliath 248, *248*
        Malaysian horned
          248–249
        poison dart 246–248,
          247
        psyllophryne didactyla
          247
        tree 246, 249
            flying 249
            red–eyed leaf 247, *247*
        whistling 248
    species of toad:
        giant or cane 246, *249,*
          249
        Surinam or pipa 248
fruit 250–251, 275–276
    avocados 251
    bananas 251
    breadfruit 251, *251*
    durian 251
    pineapples 251
    rambutan 250
fungi 240–241, 252–253, 285
    species of:
        candle snuff 253
        cookeina 252, 253
        inky caps 253
        marasmius 253
        Phillipsia cup 241
        puff balls 253
        maiden's veil stinkhorn
          253, *253*
    fungus gardens 252–253

galagos 254, 274
geckos 255–256
    dwarf 255
    flying 255, *255*
    green day 256, *256*
    leaf–tailed 256
    naked–fingered 256
    tokay 256
    turnip–tailed 256
giant otters 257, *257*
gibbons 258–259, *259*
    Kloss's 259
    siamangs 258, *258*
global warming 260–263,
    282, 291
gorillas 264–266
    mountain 264, *264*

eastern lowland 264, *265*
    western lowland 264
grasshoppers 267–269
    chlorotypus 268
    proscopia 268
    short–winged 268
    zonoceros 269
greenhouse effect 260–261
Guahibo people 289

herbivores 273–276
herbs
    lemongrass 271
    sweet basil 271
hogs 276
homes 277–281, 293
human interference 282–283
humidity 284–285
hunter–gatherers 278–279, 283,
    288–289
hydroelectricity 290–291

Ibo people 292–293, *292–293*
iguanas 294–295
    basilisk 295, *295*
    green or common 294–295,
      294
Indonesia 238

katydids 267–270, *267, 270*
    lichen 269, *269*
    mimetica incisa 270
    zabalius apicalis 270

lichens 252
light gaps 240
logging 282

marmosets and tamarins 274
Mbuti people 279, *279*, 288
millipedes 240
mining 282
monkeys 273, 276
    red colobus *273*
mosquitoes 275, 291
moss 240

oil exploration 283
orchids 285

Piaroa people 281, *281*
pigs and peccaries 276
poaching 282
pollution 238, 283, *283*
possums, honey 273, 276

rainfall 284–285, 290

reforestation 263
rhinoceroses 274

sago palm 289, *289*
scavengers 240–241
scorpions 241
seed dispersal 250–251
Semang people 289
slash and burn 262, 292
sloths 273
snails 240
soil 241, 243–244
spices
    cinnamon 272
    cloves *271*, 272
    ginger 272
    nutmeg 272
    pepper 271–272
    vanilla 272, *272*
spiders 241
squirrels 273
succession 243

tapirs 274, *275*
termites 240, 274
toads (SEE frogs and toads)
tourism 245, 266, 280, 282

viper, eyelash 287

Warrau people 289
water cycle 284–285
whip scorpions 241

Yanomami people 280
Yoruba people 279–280, 292